AGING COMES
WITHOUT A MANUAL

Scott Eubanks

STEPHEN F. AUSTIN STATE UNIVERSITY PRESS

Also by Scott Eubanks:

MAD DOGS, MARBLES, AND ROCK FIGHTS (2017)

PUBERTY DROVE THE CAR, I WAS JUST ALONG FOR THE RIDE (2020)

HOMER, a tornado wrapped in barbed wire (2021)

Managing Editor: Kimberly Verhines

Assistant Editor: Mallory LeCroy

ISBN: 978-1-62288-947-1

CONTENTS

This book is dedicated to my wife, Karen (Kay) Hightower Eubanks, the lady I have been married to for more than 57 years. She was delightful to be young with and is as much fun to be old with as she was back then. What a partner!

INTRODUCTION

I was born in 1946, making me one of the oldest of the Baby Boomers. Having studied some economics, I know all booms eventually cycle into busts. That repeating pattern does not limit itself just to the economy. It applies to people, too. I know. I know because I am now in my bust cycle, and I am smart enough to know my most productive, energetic, financially rewarding, and accomplishment-filled years are behind me. With the help of aging, a whole lot of my "want to" and "will do" has turned into "can't do." Oh, I am not saying age has caused me to want to wind-up my life, but it certainly has caused me to wind-down my life.

In prepping for writing this book, I read a lot of books and articles about aging. Most of them were written by gerontologists, medical school professors, psychiatrists, and a number of self-proclaimed "experts." The majority of the writers weren't even old when they did their writing. My primary qualification for writing this book is that I am actually old. I think my status as actually being old leaves me far from being an expert, but it does give me a certain credibility.

I heard a minister named Richard Wing remind his aging congregation that you can't practice old age. I agree with him completely. If I could have practiced old age, I would be a whole lot better at it than I am. Now, I can't honestly say getting old moved in on me all at once. There were lots of clues along the way. Things like graying hair, sagging skin, falling behind in the effort to stay technologically current, waning athletic agility, health challenges. etc., were clues that were impossible to overlook. Sagging is probably the most persistent and pervasive proof of one's aging. Everything sags more and more the older we get, from our ear lobes on down. I have so much loose skin, I give vacuum cleaners a wide birth. I came close to naming this book "The Sag Saga", but wiser heads prevailed.

Lest I forget to mention it elsewhere in this book, let me say with some conviction, old age and vanity don't fit well together. I've talked to lots of people who are in the early stages of turning golden who have assured me they WILL NOT give in to getting old. They go on to say they will fend off getting old by staying active, thinking "young", exercising, and taking vitamin supplements. I admire their feistiness and conviction, but I know they are ultimately just whistling Dixie. That same minister that said we couldn't practice for old age, also said sheer willpower makes nothing happen. The effort to ignore old age might help for a little while, but aging is a force that only death can stop. Old age is not like a fresh spring shower that leaves everything in its path brighter, healthier, and prettier. It is like an angry tsunami that sweeps over and through one's life that leaves devastation, havoc, and debris in its wake. And, oh yes, it leaves sag all over you. In his novel, EVERY CLOAK ROLLED IN BLOOD (Simon & Schuster, 2022), best-selling author James Lee Burke wrote, "age is not kind, and it leaves a mean stamp on an elderly man's perceptions."(1) I like the way Burke described one of the effects of aging on us old men. I've got the "mean stamp" markings all over my mind and body.

This book doesn't attempt to fully explain the aging process. It doesn't offer meaningful advice on how to delay the onset of oldness. Nor does it offer much advice on how to cope with getting old. It nibbles at the corners of all of these situations. However, remember the content of this book was put together by one whom is nothing more than an observer, sufferer, and a man trying to make the most out of his own aging. I do believe there is a lot of humor associated with the aging process and I have laced my stories and observations with quite a lot of it. Syndicated columnist, Froma Harrop, in a story about how the sitcom, *The Golden Girls*, dealt with aging, said it helped chase away the terrors of old age with humor. I do a little chasing here, too.

My challenge in writing this book has been to determine which direction to take it. Since I couldn't get a clear image of just one primary direction, I've written about the upsides of aging, the downsides of aging, the challenges with which we golden oldies have to deal, and some insights about old folks that younger people deal with in trying to figure out what makes old folks act like old folks.

Heck, don't over-analyze this book, just enjoy it. Dig in and grin.

OLD? WHO, ME?

"Mirror mirror on the wall. What the heck happened?"

That revelatory question is etched on a block of wood that sits where my wife, Kay, and I see it constantly. I don't know who came up with that quotable ditty, but I can guarantee you it was someone unhappy with what getting old had done to their looks. The obvious answer to the question is: we have aged, and we wear the proof of our aging on our faces and on our bodies. Our passage into old age is well-documented by our looks, our physical and mental limitations, and our ways of thinking. No one sneaks into old age. Personally, I don't think getting or being old is all that bad. It's just different. As the old saying goes, I've never been this old before. Therefore, I find the changes aging brings my way are often interesting, even humorous at times, and always new to me. Because I'm now in new territory, I have lots of new challenges and opportunities with which to deal. Some are fun; some are painful; some are sad. At this point, I am, more or less, able to focus primarily on the fun stuff.

I keep hearing that seventy is today's new fifty, or something like that. That may be true, but there really are quite a few things I can't do today that I could when I was fifty. Some survey I read on internet asked the question "when are we considered old?" The thousands that answered the survey said that men are considered old when they are seventy. Women? They are considered old when they are seventy-three.

I am now in my late 70s, but to many of my older friends, I'm still too young to have had the full force of old age bloody my nose. They say things like, "just wait" or "you won't believe the severity of the potholes in the road of life you're about to hit." I know they are right, but, at this point, I refuse to let the fear of those "bad" times ruin my enjoyment of the time I now have sitting on the throne of maturity.

The words from an old Brenda Lee song, "One Step at A Time," (2) truly sum up my current situation. The words are, "Just take one step at a time, boy, just one step at a time." That's about all any of us can do. Honestly, however, taking that next step gets a little more difficult as time passes. Ignoring old age is not an option. Dealing with it is possible. Ignoring it is not.

There's a weird website called MISTUPD.COM. It's part of the *Online Knowledge Magazine*. On it, I found several lists dealing with aging. I selected two of those listicles to share with you. The first one is called "25 Signs You Are Getting Old," (3) Here's nine of those twenty-five:

- your houseplants are alive, and you can't smoke any of them;
- having sex in a twin bed is out of the question;
- 6 AM is when you get up, not when you go to bed;
- You hear your favorite song on an elevator;
- sleeping on the couch makes your back hurt;
- you go to the drug store for anti-acid and ibuprofen, not condoms and pregnancy tests;
- you watch the weather channel;
- your friends marry and divorce rather than "hook up" and "break up;" and,
- you drink at home to save money before going to a bar.

Another pundit on that website came up with his or her own list of ways you know you are getting old. They were:

- the gleam in your eyes is from the sun hitting your bifocals;
- you sit in a rocking chair and can't get it going;
- your back goes out more than you do;
- you get your exercise acting as a pallbearer for your friends who exercise; and,
- you are asleep, but others worry you are dead.

The aging process is a sneaky son-of-a-gun. It begins by lurking around the edges of one's life and occasionally darting into your person to take a bite out of your well-being. It then zips back into the shadows and waits for the next opportunity to reappear and take another bite out of your youth, your appearance, your confidence, and or your already fragile self-concept. You'd like to grab it and strangle it, but it's always out of sight and out of reach. Each bite it takes out of one's existence leaves the victim a little less capable of ignoring the damage done by the attacks and a little less able to ignore their cumulative effects. Fighting against aging is a losing battle, but we do have a good shot at enjoying the many good parts of it.

Most of us occasionally suffer from a fear of dying. That fear may not last long, but it crosses our minds. It's logical to suffer from a fear of dying, but we should try really hard to keep that fear from causing a fear of living within us. It may be a fate worse than death to go through life afraid of living.

Mort, a dear friend of mine who is in his eighties, bought himself a new Mercedes that happens to be the fastest model they have ever produced. He didn't tell me how much it cost, but I am certain it priced out at *too-much-ninety-five*. Mercedes produced a very small number of these jets on four wheels and because he has bought a new racing model from them every time they've come up with a newer and faster one, he was on their approved buyer list. Mort picked me up in his new car for a quick demo drive, and after about a ten-minute ride he brought me back to my business. During the test run, he never drove over seven or eight miles per hour, so I asked him why he bought the fastest car on the highway if he was never going to break the ten mile per hour barrier. He said it was because he liked knowing he could if he wanted to. He then explained that at his age, there were very few vices still available to him. A fast car was one. I told him he should get a speeding ticket, because, at his age, it would look good on his resume.

Another friend of mine named Bill Schultz recently passed away at 104 years old. He was still as sharp as a tack right up until his last week or so. He drove everywhere he went and had looks that belied his real age by at least 30-35 years. The last time we spoke, I asked him if he still swam thirty minutes every day. He answered, "No. It's too damned much trouble." I then asked him if he still had his martini every day. He responded, "Yes. It's no trouble at all."

A feisty little lady named Miss Bessie Bryant taught elementary school in my hometown of Marshall, Texas for more than fifty years. When she turned 102, her family checked her into a nursing home. One day I accompanied my oldest brother and one of my uncles on a visit to another resident in Miss Bessie's nursing home. My brother and my uncle had been in Miss Bessie's first grade class many, many years before. As we walked down the wide hallway, a firm feminine voice in a room we were passing said, "Aren't you boys going to stop and say hello to your first-grade teacher?" Miss Bessie had recognized both men and pounced on them for passing her by. We reversed gears and stepped into her room. She not only recognized both "boys", but she also told them exactly where they had sat in her class. She then told my uncle that he had been a real handful (he never grew out of that) and told my brother that he was a daydreamer who spent most of his class time staring out of the window (he never grew out of that either).

I have shared these three stories to remind us that life and the plea sures it provides don't stop at the same time for everyone. Some brains and memories stay sharp for ages and ages. Factors such as good genetics, life-styles, fast cars, and martinis helps some folks stretch their pleasures much longer into old age.

When groups of oldsters engage in unstructured discussions, they often question each other about how they feel about dying. The most common answer I've heard to that question is, "I don't fear dying, but I do fear the act of dying." That answer makes sense to me. No one invites pain into their life, and there's a prevalent suspicion that the act of dying is painful. We don't know if it is or isn't. These discussions usually get around to question-ing whether or not we are met by a bright light with images of loved ones that have already "crossed over." We have all heard stories about someone who "died" on the operating table but miraculously came back to like. They usually tell the bright light/loved ones story. A friend of ours named Carol told us she was in an automobile accident in Texas and hovering on the edge of death when she was physically pulled to safety from the burning wreckage by an angel—a real angel. She saw the angel and knew she had been saved by an act of God. One can only wonder and hope. By the way, Carol hasn't missed church since her personal miracle.

When I was only in my late fifties, I wasn't oblivious to my aging, but I was handling the process with relative ease. I felt good, handled my mental challenges with aplomb, and thought I still looked pretty good. I was coping. Then one night, the ogre of aging reared its head and slapped me right across my ego. It happened when I came home from an exhausting day of work. I was spent, and my condition was emphasized by my slumped shoulders, tired eyes, and whipped-puppy attitude. While in the bathroom washing up for supper, I looked in the mirror and found an old man staring back at me—a man I didn't remember seeing before. Feeling sorry for myself, I sought out my wife, certain she would pump-up my lagging confidence by assuring me I was still on top of my game. I plopped down beside her on the sofa and in my most pathetic voice, asked her, "Kay, how long have I looked this old?" She looked at me, thought for a second or two, and calmly answered, "Oh, I'd say seven or eight years."

She wasn't kidding. She was serious, and I was shocked. Here I had just begged her for a compliment to help me restore my battered ego, and she inflicted me with the staggering truth and delivered it with the finesse of a D-9 Caterpillar. Wham! Not what I wanted to hear from my loving wife, and not what I expected. She passed over the chance to offer restorative words and opted to give me a major shove down the road to old age on which I now traveled. While the re-telling of this story hardly puts me in the mood to defend my wife, I feel it only fair to admit that I had learned many years ago to never ask Kay a question unless I was prepared for the unvarnished truth. While I think my question to her called for a little spousal sensitivity, it's hard to argue with the truth. I had obviously starting "wearing" my age well before I recognized it in myself.

If I had to pinpoint one incident that caused me to realize my senior status was upon me and my youth was in my rearview mirror, it was that one. The race to old age was on, and I was run over by the power and speed of the assault on my youth that now had the pedal to the metal. I'm surprised—and a bit disappointed—it didn't take longer to get old.

Many of the questions we seniors ask about our appearance, mental acumen, or philosophies are really put out there in search of compliments. The truth hurts and we have no desire to hurt ourselves. I do not mind being lied to when I throw out these opportunities to compliment me. Kay is not like that. I am.

You've probably noticed that I like using lists in this book. They are easy to find and tell the story of our aging quite nicely. I've run across lots of lists and commentaries dealing with how we can tell we are aging. It's harder to find lists that tell us how we can know we are old. A middle-aged writer named Natalie Romero gave us a list sharing her personal observations about getting older. Seven of the items listed in her article, "Ten Unmistakable Signs You are Getting Old," (4) are as follows:

- sometimes when I open my mouth, my mother comes out;
- stray hairs;
- my pee;
- my stiffness;
- I don't understand the music;
- my going to bed early; and,
- retirement condos sound appealing.

Her list may be a little offbeat, but it clearly has a ring of truth to it and it hit some things I had not thought of.

Getting old is very different from being old. Now, once we have moved beyond enumerating the things to watch out for as we track our aging, *The Coventry Telegraph* ran an article entitled, "The Top 50 Signs You're Old." (5)

They skipped right over listing the things that might mean you are getting old and went to the "You are old if…" part. Look at the ten of these items I chose to list and decide if the shoe of old age fits. Here we go:

- forgetting people's names;
- losing hair;
- feeling stiff;
- talking a lot about your ailments;
- groaning when you bend down;
- sagging;
- misplacing your glasses, car keys, etc.;
- getting more hairy—ears, nose, eyebrows, face, etc.;
- avoid lifting anything heavy due to a back concern; and,
- saying, "in my day."

The article went on to point out that these symptoms start exhibiting themselves at age 41.

I really didn't need all of these lists and all of this prose to know that I am old. It may be of more value to those who are getting old or are curious about what it's like to be old. The title of this chapter is, "OLD? WHO, ME?" As I've written it, I've answered those questions for myself. Yes, I am old.

QUESTIONS I WANT TO ASK GOD

I think the biggest and most important question any human being wants an answer to has to be, "Is there a God?" Many factors in our lives determine on what answer we place our chips. Were we raised to believe? Were we raised to be non-believers? Were we raised in an environment that left it up to us individually to make up our own minds? Some people claim to be atheists and others claim to be agnostic. They are still trying to decide what they believe. Those who believe are said to have faith and, as we all know, faith is only needed in the absence of certainty.

Certainty is not easy to find in religion. There are forty thousand Christian denominations (give or take a few thousand) in the world and lots of other belief systems that have different gods and objects to worship. The Christian denominations are bound by a shared belief in Jesus Christ. They are separated by different interpretations of the teachings in the Bible. If all those students of the Word can't reach agreement, it's to be expected that us non-clergy pew birds have lots of questions, most of which only God can answer.

My faith meter is perched right near the "full" indicator. I'm a believer. However, whether you are a believer or not, there must be questions you would like to ask God if He turns outs to be real. It would be easy to fill a boxcar with theological and "how did you…" scientific questions, but those aren't the kinds of questions I had in mind when I started this chapter. I figure that if we are to enjoy eternal life in God's heaven, He will have plenty of time to answer those complicated, technical posers. I even suspect a lot of those questions will be answered in an orientation class for Heaven newbies. Here, I hope to come up with some seldom-thought-of questions that may put a smile on God's lips. For example:

- Do you have ice cream and gravy in Heaven?
- What's up with roaches, flies, and mosquitos?
- Do animals know of you?
- Do you favor either of your parents?
- Why do men have teats? Are they part of Your future plans?
- My friend Ronnie wants to know if you have a room full of angels that help you answer all of the prayers humans offer up.

- Did you create platypuses and orangutans when you were in a silly mood?
- Robert Henry, who passed away years ago in Dallas, told his daughter Nancy he always wondered why God took his teeth and left him his testicles, adding he could have used his teeth in old age.
- Did the disciples have nicknames, i.e., was Peter called Pete? Was Matthew called Matty?
- My wife wants to know why women have hot flashes.
- I read about a woman on *cafemom.com* who wants to ask God, "Why do you make women have menstrual cycles when other advanced species don't have them?"
- Who were your parents?
- Are there hospitals in heaven for the spiritually ill?
- Do you ever get bored?
- Was man's inability to get along with other men the result of a design flaw?
- Do you re-cycle souls?
- Do people take naps in Heaven?
- Why are avocado pits so large?
- Do you have any hobbies?
- What do you do for fun?
- Do you have any close friends?
- Eternity is a long time. Do any Heaven-dwellers get bored?
- What makes you mad at Heaven-dwellers?
- Where did the color maroon go?
- Are there other gods for other worlds? If so, do you know them?
- Is there a pecking order in Heaven?
- What do you eat?
- Is time measured in Heaven?
- What was your most useless creation? (Please don't say me.)
- What did you do before you created the world and us? Were you in God school learning how to do all of that creating?
- Do you go on vacation, and, if so, where do you go, and who do you leave in charge?
- What gets you tickled?
- Have you ever had a date?
- Does it bother you that Mother Nature gets praised for the beauty you created?

• Does being asked stupid questions bug you?

Many of you will remember Art Linkletter's television show called "House Party" that ran on radio and television in the 1940s and 1950s. It had a segment named "Kids Say the Darndest Things" in which he asked young children various questions. Their answers were usually unexpected and downright hilarious. Years later, Bill Cosby hosted a television program with the same name and the results were the same. Kids still gave us surprising and funny answers. They still do. When a group of youngsters were given the chance to ask God questions, they surprised us again. Here are a few of their questions for God, courtesy of cafemom.com (6):

• Did Jesus have to be potty trained?
• Is Santa your rich brother?
• If you see everything, do you watch us in the shower?
• Is Jesus a zombie?
• If Jesus doesn't have a sister, why do I have to have one?

Can't you just imagine our all-powerful God smiling and shaking his head as he heard those questions?

I hope no hardliner believes I am being insulting to God. I mean no disrespect. I'm just using the curiosity God planted in my brain. I know God has a sense of humor, or he would not have designed the aging process as he did. Also, this awesome force is the same fellow that created camels, platypuses, orangutans, freckles, hairless cats and dogs, cross-eyed mules, buzzards, and fainting goats.

CHANGE? CHANGE? BAH HUMBUG!

"Change is inevitable, except from a vending machine."
–Anonymous.

The older I get the more I tend to look back at what I credit with be-ing kinder and gentler times. I have found it rather easy to forget Charles Manson, bigotry, Vietnam, the emergence of the drug culture, gang violence, Watergate, Chappaquiddick, and the assassinations of John F. Kennedy, Medgar Evers, Martin Luther King, Bobby Kennedy, and Malcolm X that occurred while my generation was on watch. Kinder and gentler? Really? I guess what I am saying is that every generation has good things and bad things about it. In my case, the older I get, the more my memory seems to focus on the good stuff. Maybe that's a way God eases us into readiness for our end times.

I believe change is occurring so rapidly today it is impossible to write a definitive paper or book on the subject. By the time the writer puts his last period in place, so much has changed since he started his writing, his thoughts are passé. While efforts to quantify change are virtually impossible, there are kinds of changes we can discuss. For example, we all know things cost more today. We all know music has gone "downhill" dramatically since "our" music faded away alongside the record player. By the way, if you're holding your breath waiting for an elderly person to tell you he/she likes rap music, prepare for what I believe will be a long, long wait. Oh some will admit they like it, but it's likely to be a small few. I could never convince my parent's generation that rock and roll was fabulous, and rap lovers will have a lot of trouble selling the merits of rap to my generation Age, too often, causes us to be less adaptable than we should be.

Those same elderly folks I mentioned in the previous chapter are also likely to give a big thumbs down to the wearing of saggy/baggy pants that reveal bits of butt crack and the wearer's undies as well as most tattoos. They will also tell you television was classier when Rob and Laura Petrie slept in separate beds on *The Dick Van Dyke Show* and that it has moral-ly regressed by airing today's sex-charged dramas. Inuendo worked for us. Judging by the content of today's movies and television shows, marriage is just an option now, not a logical step to be taken by those in love. Today's practice of show it, tell it, and do it, leaves little need for imagination. We like/liked sex as much as any generation. We just preferred it in privacy. Many of the changes we frown upon are really just irritating to us, not earth-shattering catastrophes. They just rock our world, not upend it.

I am inclined to believe when a generation gets old, it sort of feels as though the generation replacing it is botching things up a bit and straying from propriety. We have to feel that way as a means of validating our own time on earth. I am confident every generation has had its doubts as it passed the baton to the next generation. I know my dad felt as though he and Mother were too soft on my two brothers and me. He feared their coddling of us might leave us ill-equipped to handle the hard side of life when we grew up. He only half-jokingly accused Mother of "mommynizing" us boys. She did.

When "change" is the subject, a writer can go in myriad directions. By definition, change is endless. Knowing I cannot adequately cover the subject, I opt to mention just a few changes that speak volumes about the differences between my generation and the one nudging me out the door.

The *Andy Griffith Show* was a wonderful example of much of my generation's television. It was simple, clean, wholesome, funny, and instructional on how to live our lives with character. We all knew Opie would grow up to be a fine human being because he was wrapped in the fabric of good character by his patient, loving father Andy and his doting Aunt Bee. Heck, all of Mayberry participated in raising Opie. In it, honesty, morality, and good character were rewarded with happiness, a loving hug, and, quite often, with a slice of Aunt Bea's apple pie.. Those positive traits were expected of Opie, and he was not rewarded for doing what was right, just punished for doing what was wrong. I think if the *Andy Griffith Show* was on today's prime time line-up, it would be completely different. I think Andy would be a sleep-around stud, Barney would be a lovable pervert, Aunt Bee would be sneaking around with Floyd the barber, Howard would be a cross dresser, Ernest T. Bass would be a flasher, and Opie would be fighting an opioid addiction, and the word shucks" would be replaced with the word "shit." Think about it. What moral lessons are we passing on with shows like *Two and a Half Men*, *Naked and Afraid*, *Family Guy*, and *Keeping Up with the Kardashians*? A moron can see that nearly every movie or television show totally discards the need for marriage in any relationship and includes a healthy dose of meaningless, uncomplicated, ultra-casual sex. I'm not a prude. Nor am I guiltless. I do, however, think many of the changes our society has undergone in recent years are shortsighted and may prove costly to future generations. Time will tell. I won't be here to say, "I told you so," but, as I said, time will tell.

Remember that song, "I Saw Mommy Kissing Santa Claus" (underneath the mistletoe last night)? It was a hit record in 1952. I opine that if it were recorded today, it would be amended to include lyrics about Daddy following up the incident by murdering Santa Claus.

Without a doubt, the shooting of Santa would "trigger" the re-emergence of a loud call for the repeal of the Second Amendment. To counteract this movement to de-weaponize America, our computers would hum with emails from gun advocates defending the Second Amendment. One thing's for certain, the kiss under the mistletoe would be hailed as a sex scandal, and it and Santa's murder would go viral on social media within an hour.

"Frosty the Snowman" was one of my favorite Christmas stories. If it were re-released and contemporized, I think it would be quite different from the old original version. Instead of just melting from the weather warming up, I think Frosty may have fallen victim to a serial thawer. The evildoer would go on to thaw Alaska and a number of major icebergs before he was finally imprisoned in an ice cube by Commander Chill, a new and powerful superhero who lives secretly in an abandoned ice house in Woonsocket, Rhode island. At the very least, half of the politicians would blame Frosty's demise on global warming.

What about the story of Rudolph the Red-Nosed Reindeer? If rewritten today, Rudolph would sue all of the other reindeer and Mr. and Mrs. Santa Claus for cruelty and persecution. He would win the case and people would take to the streets, set fires, break some windows, and do a little looting to celebrate their court victory.

I thought the idea of re-writing some of the sweet old children's stories with a contemporary slant might be a good way to illustrate how things have changed in the past 50 years. My enthusiasm for doing so was dampened somewhat when my son told me Warner Brothers beat me to the idea by creating and releasing a Christmas cartoon called "A Miser Brothers' Christmas" in 2008. In it, Snow Miser and Heat Miser, feuding sons of Mother Nature, are forced to work together in order to save Christmas. The kid-friendly animation doesn't involve serious evil or violence, but it does stray from the traditional happy kiddie story.

Also, when I was a young boy, I remember watching a segment on *The Bullwinkle Show* called "Fractured Fairy Tales." Author A. J. Jacobs took charming fairy tales and bedtime stories and warped and twisted them into weird tales Mother Goose would have never recognized. Clearly, Jacobs created his odd stories before political correctness ruled the day.

Back to reality. I liked my world when I was underinformed. I really didn't need to know President Eisenhower had a girlfriend or that President Kennedy had lots of them. They were my presidents, not my priests. Social media itself doesn't bug me. The fact that people can't stay off of it drives me nuts. To me, it seems the overwhelming majority of what appears on social media is needless information and smells of garbage. Do people really think others care what they had for dinner or what their opinion is of the dress a classmate wore to the dance? Get a clue.

I read that pornography comprises 60% of the web's content. If that figure is anywhere close to accurate, then my claim of it being filled with garbage rings true. If we add all of the twisted and exaggerated political information that circulates on the web to its porn content, we could realistically question the value of the web and certainly social media to the good of mankind.

I am probably operating from the assumption that if I don't understand it, it must be bad, but I just don't see the merits of social media. I think it should be put in the category of a "social disease" rather than a form of media. Oh my, this editorializing is so much fun. It has to be therapeutic for me to get these opinions off my chest. I do, however, realize these somewhat provincial and rather dated ideas I am advancing could easily mark me as a grouchy old man. If I have earned that label, I will wear it with a sense of inevitability. Remember, this book is about aging, not right or wrong, not good or bad. It's just a take on what I—an old man—see and feel today compared with what I saw and felt years ago.

As I just reminded you, this book is about aging. So far, I've liked every age I've been. I even like getting old. I like that my old age allows me more latitude in voicing my opinions and causes others to accept my being grouchy and set in my ways. It seems to me many younger people expect those traits in older folks so it's no big deal when I fulfill their expectations. Much of our lives is spent trying to please others and trying to measure up to the expectations with which we've been saddled by someone else. In old age, posturing for society is over and done. We can now shoot from the hip for the most part. Bang! Though we still have to choose our words carefully lest we do serious harm to another person. Stray verbal bullets can be fatal to a relationship.

The power of words and our sensitivities to them was illustrated to me a couple of years ago at my granddaughter's high school volleyball game. It was played in our home gym and our student spectators were really into it. They were loud in their support of the Arcadia Titans. I couldn't discern what they were yelling at the other team, but, apparently, someone took offense. The referees stopped the match two times to have certain students removed from the gym for whatever they were hollering. When they had to stop play for a third time, the refs instructed the students to refrain from yelling anything "negative" to the visiting team.

When I realized it was the parents and grandparents, not the students, who groaned and voiced their disapproval of the mandate to the referees, it struck me as an example of the generational differences between the old and the young. The older folks were up in arms that the referee was so protective of the feeling of girls being yelled at. They did not approve of the efforts to insulate the kids from criticism. Us older folks grew up in a time when not everyone made a sports team. It was a time when if a kid didn't have the requisite talent to help a team, they were cut and had to find another sport or hobby. There certainly weren't "participation" trophies given to everyone who showed up. The parents and grandparents did not raise hell with the league because their child was cut. The act was viewed as a learning experience that would pay dividends in the long run. I will not defend the way we grew up. It may or may not have been superior to the current system of declaring everyone a winner. Lordy, everyone these days seems so sensitive. They even appear as though they are walking around in search of being offended. I don't know. That night at the gym, I just noted the change, and change is what this chapter is all about.

In writing the above paragraph, I remembered another sports incident involving my son Paul that now serves as an example of the changes that have occurred in recent years. It was 1982, and we lived in Barrington, Rhode Island. Paul was a highly competitive 12-year-old little leaguer who was not used to making outs. One night, he ended the game by grounding out in a critical situation. As he crossed first base, he yelled out the f-word in anger at himself. He was normally a reserved, rather quiet kid, so his outburst took everyone by surprise. When we got home that evening, I made him call all of the parents who were in the grandstand next to where his eruption occurred and apologize for his profanity and poor sportsmanship. He reluctantly did so, but much to my surprise, most of those he called just laughed off the incident and couldn't believe I had made him call and apologize. That incident left me fairly certain that I was one of the last of a breed that held so tightly to outdated social mores. Today, many younger people feel right at home swearing in public and around their parents. They may be comfortable within the new lax behavioral environment, but I'm not there yet.

While old age brings certain freedoms with it, it does not mean we will—or even could—completely break with traditions, old habits, and societal expectations. I've always fancied myself as one comfortable with a bit of nonconformity and as one unafraid to take the road less traveled. In truth, I've probably been as bound to convention as the next guy and predictably so. I was raised that way. I tried to live up to what was expected of me. Even in old age, I'm probably not the rebel I claim to be. Just yesterday, I was dressing for a lunch date with friends when I got the urge to wear a purple shirt with dark green pants. I wanted to be unconventional and sartorially daring. Couldn't do it. I chickened out and put on a white polo. I hate disappointing myself. We can't fight who we really are. I've basically been a rule follower all of my life. There's little chance I will change my style of living late in life.

I think most of us traditionalists have a rebellious side we bury deep within ourselves. We may want to turn it loose, but our acquired desire to fit in keeps it in check. You may have noticed that wearing crazy socks is all the fad today. I think it may be because doing so lets us lightly scratch our itch to rebel without flaunting it. Wearing Sasquatch socks is timid enough to do. Wearing Sasquatch pants would be too daring and may focus ridicule on us. We are just too chicken to be too bold.

I've noticed an interesting drama play out in my son's household regarding the length of his hair. He let his hair grow quite long recently and his teenaged daughters loved it, as did quite a few of his female clients. His wife told him to do what he wanted to do, but her disapproval of his flowing locks was apparent. He knew we parents thought he "looked better" with a more conventional haircut. He struggled between going rogue and going conservative. He ultimately elected to lop off his long hair. Knowing my son as I do, I'll bet his long hair reappears in the not-too-distant future.

Have you noticed we all like movie and television heroes who disregard the rules in order to achieve their goals? I think our fondness for the rule breakers may be a way we protest our own conventionality. To an extent, we live vicariously through their boldness. Movies, books, and television shows allow us to escape our self-imposed practicality. A little bit of James Thurber's character Walter Mitty lives in all of us. I must confess. I love the movies in which Clint Eastwood or Charles Bronson just shoots the bad guy. That just "makes my day."

There are all sorts of concessions we make to getting old. At some point in time, we have to accept our slowness, the loss of our quickness of body and mind, the awkward stiffness that has replaced our agility, the diminution and ultimate loss of our sex lives, and the reliability of our senses and bodily functions. If we live long enough, we embrace our dependence on help-aids like walking canes, walkers, wheelchairs, stool softeners, pacemakers, hearing aids, glasses, and c-pap machines. They just become part of our lives—things that keep us going. They are godsends, not nuisances. They are symbols of the changes that affect our lives as we get older. They are also proof of the fact that we are hanging in there. Our spry may have sprung, but don't count us out.

I read a letter to the editor in today's newspaper that reminded me of another change I don't like. In it, an elderly man complained that when he calls a technology help desk, his call is immediately switched to a help tech located in the Philippines, India, or some other country that struggles with speaking understandable English. The letter writer asserts that the simple transfer of his call to a workroom in some foreign nation with an inferior telecommunications system causes a 30% drop in the volume with which his discussion will be conducted. He goes on to write that, at his age, he needs more volume, not less. He further states rather emphatically that the combination of low volume and poor enunciation of the English language by the foreign techs exacerbates his old age hearing deficiencies and renders his call for help totally useless. My wife and I read his letter together, then gave the elderly writer a big thumbs up. Write on and right on fellow warrior! I would like to add that I am amazed how many of these foreign, non-understandable techies claim their name is Jerry, Kevin, Larry, or Lucy. Now understand me before you jump down my throat. I DO NOT blame the foreign techies. They are trying to make a living and I applaud their efforts. I DO blame American companies and call centers for sacrificing their quality customer service to save a few bucks. Their obvious effort at defusing our discomfort with talking to someone in a foreign nation by adopting an American name only puts a fine edge on my anger and unhappiness. Have you noticed what a relief it is when any of your telephone inquiries are handled by an understandable English speaker? Now, in a spirit of full disclosure, I must confess that sometimes American folks who live up North struggle with understanding my East Texas/Southern drawl. We usually work out our verbal differences amicably before shots are fired.

Realizing the inevitability of change is one of the most difficult parts of getting old. While there are still many, many fun and useful things we can do as older folks, we are ever cognizant of the growing list of things we can no longer do. That's tough.

We don't seem able to adapt to change as easily or rapidly as we once did. We are often overwhelmed by the changes we are asked to accept. Many of the changes represent the unknown to us, and the unknown can be frightening to anyone, regardless of his or her age. If you are still in the prime of your life, you have surely seen the strange look on an older person's face when the discussion turns to technological advancements in our lives. That look is a mixture of confoundment, futility, frustration, hostility, embarrassment, and a bit of anger. Just when we finally learned to email, technology took 15 quantum leaps in all technological directions leaving us in the ashes of ignorance. Since I clearly don't understand how social media works, I am inclined to question its value, and I bash it every chance I get. I have concluded that if I don't understand it or use it, it's useless. Defense mechanism? Probably.

My smartphone and I don't have a meaningful relationship. I don't know enough of its capabilities to use it much. I don't just constantly stare at it like so many younger people do. I don't panic if I go somewhere and leave it at home. I don't find it thrilling that a small harmless looking machine is smarter than I am. I was happy with dumb phones. We were on the same wave length and shared the same I.Q. Another thing to remember is that any and all of my accomplishments were achieved without the aid of smart phones. If you do catch me staring at my cell phone, chances are I am just contemplating how far I could throw that electronic s.o.b.

Rapid technological changes have given birth to a new disease. It's called technophobia. One develops this new malady by being unable to understand how to use computers and other electronic devices. Sufferers are dizzied by the rapidity of the changes that affect the machines. Also, their feelings of hopelessness are compounded by their inability to stay up with technology. I sometimes wonder who canceled my DSL and stole my memory card. I seldom admit this, but I think my Google has turned to Gaggle. I spend a lot of time seated at my computer wondering: *what do I do now?*

In extreme cases, technophobes develop a hatred for all things electronic. Like most diseases, technophobia is rougher on old people whose coping abilities are already damaged by slowness, indecision, and a general lack of confidence, than it is on youngsters. While technophobia is an acknowledged health problem, I suggest we might add diseases with names like "rapid onset technitis", "electronic rejection syndrome", and "electronic-inspired hysteria." The problems are real, and the symptoms leading up to them have been identified by a growing number of researchers.

- rampant hives caused by touching computers, smart phones, or remote controls of any kind;
- dramatic seizures caused by a younger person's effort to explain a new technology;
- a nervous breakdown caused by trying to remember which password works where;
- brief comas caused by overload of electronic information;
- electronic frustration infused bouts of uncontrollable sobbing;
- sudden outbreaks of frustration and anger that may include giving the world and everyone in it the middle finger;
- attempted suicides fueled by the feeling of ignorance instilled by not being able to grasp technology; and,
- self-imposed solitary confinement in a closet, tall tree, or car trunk, triggered by the ringing of a smart phone.

I thought I would have some fun talking about the weird health issues that may affect young people someday if they continue to text and play games on their phones. I was going to make up symptoms and come up with some witty names for the new diseases I foresaw on the horizon. Guess what? I'm too late. There are already many health issues that have been identified as being the result of too much texting, gaming, and looking down at electronic devices. The problems are real, and the symptoms leading up to them have been identified through extensive clinical research. [Note: To make a claim that extensive clinical research has revealed these issues, you need to source clinical research. Your listed sources are not] A whole new compendium of technology-related medical jargon is in the books. Ever heard of these new "diseases" that are beginning to aggressively affect our young people? (7)

- text neck—generally caused by looking down at our phones too much;
- carpal tunnel syndrome—pain, numbness, and weakness in wrist caused by repetitive motions like texting;
- numb thumbs—a pinched nerve caused by overuse of thumbs, such as in texting and gaming;

- selfie elbow—self-explanatory;
- neck humps—a deformity caused by looking down too much;
- computer vision syndrome—occurs when too much time is spent looking at small screens; sometimes referred to as eye strain.
- detached retinas—caused by too much screen time;
- gamer's thumb—similar to numb thumbs; and,
- text claw—misshaped hands and fingers caused by too much texting/ gaming.

I am certain there are other maladies that should be added to this list, but I've listed enough to illustrate the problems some of our technological advancements have left for us to sort out. Someday soon there will be a medical specialty that focuses on dealing with technology related illnesses. Maybe there already is. While all of these medical issues are troublesome, let's also acknowledge that we lose something else by allowing a generation to grow up with a severely fractured ability to converse face to face with other humans.

I can easily imagine the United States government and its National Institute of Health, aided by the Center for Disease Control in Atlanta, spending billions on researching for cures of these "new" diseases but being unable to come up with a vaccine(s). A very fanciful possibility is that maybe someone with an abundance of unused property will step into the breech and build off-the-grid retreats throughout the country where those suffering from Technophobia or any of its offshoots can hide out and exist in an environment that has no electronic machines, devices, or telephones. The total absence of these ringing, beeping, blinking, whirring things will offer the afflicted a chance at rehabilitation, but the recidivism rate will likely be quite high among those re-entering our technology-based society. I know the scenario I've spelled out sounds rather far-fetched, but so did Orwell's "1984" when it was first published. We'll see.

As old age invades our space, change comes at us at mind-bending speed. Our first reaction is to resent it and fight it. As we calm down a bit, we begin to accept its inevitability and try to roll with it. Once we realize we cannot stop it or even slow it down, it can actually be fun to just watch it happen. It's an amazing spectacle that seems to keep the world on edge and chasing its own tail. I somewhat enjoy the show, particularly since I'm at the age I can just ignore it if I'm happy with my status quo.

I've always heard styles come, go, and return a few years down the road. I haven't found that to be the case except in men's ties. Car styles of the 50s with all the fins, white wall tires, and dramatic chrome haven't returned. Leisure suits haven't re-emerged as big sellers, although I now hear they go for big money in retro or classic clothes shops. Even if they had come back in style, I wouldn't have been able to wear them. My physique and waistline have "matured" over time. Anyone want a puka shell necklace? White socks with loafers aren't the rage today they were in the 50s and 60s, but who cares? My editor informs me puka shell necklaces and white socks with loafers are actually current 2023 trends for young women. I repeat, who cares? Style changes don't really matter. No one, not even senior citizens, get their bowels in an uproar when changes happen at this level.

It's different when changes involve society, morals, character, integrity, and lawfulness. These changes can be great and cause for celebration if they strengthen any of those societal traits. If, instead, they degrade any of the standards we hope for in those societal traits, we should be concerned, worried, and prayerful. Older people are the perfect judges of the value or damage major changes cause to our collective ethos. Why? Our generation has lived through multiple generations and has a basis for comparing the standards each generation assigned to itself. The younger folks who are living through society today have no basis with which to compare the behavioral standards by which they are judged. It's their first time at the rodeo. Many young people think of their grandparents and other older people as yesterday's news because their thoughts and social commentaries are out-of-touch with what's hip today. In my case, I'm guilty as charged. It's really not fair of me to superimpose my generation's rules on the next batch of human beings. It is, however, fair for me to voice my opinions, shake my head in disbelief, and worry about what I perceive to be a permissiveness that moves our people further from what is important in life. Grumble, grumble. I suspect these last two or three paragraphs leave little doubt that I'm a voting member of the Old Farts' Club.

As a society, we generally upgrade through change. As stated before, we cannot reject change, only resist it. We golden agers would do well to focus on what we will gain from change, not what we will have to give up. However, we should choose the changes we endorse very carefully. Not all changes advance our well-being. We should let positive change feed a new part of our being; let it fuel growth and renewal within us. I would add that not all change is necessary either. My unsolicited advice is pretty simple. Embrace the good change. Flush the bad change.

AN OLD MAN'S URGES

When I was younger, I was filled with urges. They burned in my mind and body and strained against the confines in which I tried to live. They often wanted to jump out of my skin and run free through opportunities they perceived as reachable and doable. My urges were fueled by self-confidence, energy, curiosity, ambition, and a love of adventure. Before your imagination gets away from you, let me assure you my urges extended far beyond those of a sexual nature, and most of them were sheer fantasy. I dealt with personal urges that—if acted upon—included career changes, living in countless communities I found inviting, running for political office, and speaking my mind irreverently in situations normally imbued with passivity. I even had the urge to organize an army for the purpose of overthrowing the government of Madagascar. By taking over that defenseless, poverty-stricken country, I would have been able to set up a new government that was built on fairness and love for all people. Vanilla beans would have been our monetary unit, and the export of it would have provided our economic strength. Now that would have been challenging and fun. Those sorts of urges were hallmarks of my youth.

Now that I am in my 70s, I still have urges. They are vastly different from the urges of my youth but urges just the same. I read and hear a lot about older folks developing a "bucket list," i.e., a list of things they want to do before they give up the ghost. I don't think of the urges listed below as things I have to do, I just think they would be fun. Here are some of this old man's urges:

- I would like to speed through Colorado and Oregon putting Republican Party bumper stickers on all the Subarus I run across;
- I would like to make obscene gestures to all those I see throwing cigarette butts out their car windows onto the street;
- I would like to walk into a Texas honkytonk and announce that the guy who parked his pick-up truck in the gravel parking lot needs to rush home because his wife's in bed with his friend. I'd have to press against the wall to keep from getting trampled;
- I would like to commandeer the public address system at a rodeo and

announce that John Wayne was gay just to witness the attack the cow-boys would muster for trying to capture and hog tie yours truly;

- I would like to tell women in the grocery store check-out line not to buy the trashy magazine they're flipping through and remind them the grocery store has not replaced the public library in America...yet;
- I have the urge to ask people what possessed them to color their bodies with multiple tattoos;
- I would like to tell pot-bellied old men how silly they look wearing a do-rag (instead of a helmet) sitting astride a big Harley;
- I would like to feel free to throw away a tube of toothpaste before I've squeezed it so much my fingers hurt;
- I would like to eat all the good stuff I did before I had heart surgery and type 2 diabetes;
- I would like to re-write the American penal code and add crime-appropriate punishments for felons such as pedophiles, those who defraud the elderly and the ignorant, and politicians and bureaucrats who steal from the public; and,
- I still have the urge take control of Madagascar by coup.

Think about my list of urges. It might be fun for you to make your own list. It could even be therapeutic. I do know I am somewhat stuck in the old school when it comes to fads and fashions such as tattoos and and tabloids at the check-out lines at supermarkets. Don't waste your precious time being upset with my musings.

Urges are part of the human experience. Whether we are talking about bodily urges, urges to break away from convention, or urges born from our suppressed frustrations, we are generally full of urges. Most of my youthful urges fell in the category of "I wish I could...." Most of my old man urges start with "I wish I STILL could..." For the most part, my brain and my body have stayed in sync with each other as I have aged. That's not always the case when it comes to dealing with urges. My brain still comes up with some real doozies in terms of urges and desires. My body quickly rejects most of those fantasies. However, I should let you know I still enjoy the dickens out of some of my exciting urges, even if I don't spend a lot of time seriously contemplating how to implement them. I find a creative mind can provide endless hours of entertainment and, at this age, the list of things I find entertaining is dwindling rapidly.

I have noticed several urges, or perhaps they are better described as tendencies, in some older people I just cannot understand. A few of those puzzlers are:

- a tendency to talk to one's self, or at least mumble just below the hearable level. One such mumbler advised me that talking to herself was the only way she could enjoy an intelligent conversation;
- a tendency to buy white, four-door Buicks;
- a tendency to put ball caps and a box of Kleenex in the rear window of their Buick;
- a tendency for old men to wear knee-length black nylon compression socks with their walking shorts (a bad look, gentlemen);
- a tendency for some old men to cede the car driving responsibilities to their wives (I'm almost there);
- a tendency for old men to hang out near the donuts; and,
- a tendency to "need" certain things that are familiar to them such as their own pillow, their own toilet seat, their favorite coffee mug, and a certain brand of toilet paper.

I know those around me would love an opportunity to throttle me because they take offense at my list of confounding and irksome urges and tendencies. Okay.

The urge to buy a Buick late in life has long been a mystery to me. I've about decided people of my vintage probably grew up in families that bought Fords, Chevrolets, and Plymouths. Cadillacs, Chryslers, and Lincolns were just monetarily out of reach for most working families. Buicks, Oldsmobiles, and Pontiacs were a step up, but still financially out of reach for many folks. The owner of one of these cars was generally considered successful, and the cars were thought of as somewhat luxurious. Cars were—and remain today—a bit of a status symbol. I think, subconsciously, many older Americans, who still have to watch their pennies, feel as though they are rewarding themselves for a life well-lived by buying a Buick. Pontiacs and Oldsmobiles are no longer manufactured. They believe they have earned a step-up, and Buick fits the bill. Just a theory. By the way, foreign jewels like Mercedes Benz, Jaguar, BMW, Audi, Lexus, Infinity, and Genesis just weren't around in most American towns and cities back in the 50s and 60s. I have no theory as to why old people like to put their caps and a box of Kleenex in their rear windows. Oh well, it beats the hell out of beanie babies.

As to why so many older men yield the steering wheel to their spouses, it might be as simple as they have become bad drivers and are smart enough to recognize that fact. It could also be that it has become easier to let a wife drive than it is to listen to her complaining about your bad driving. The last possible theory I will advance on this subject is that the man, who is usually older than his wife, is just plain worn out and welcomes the opportunity to shed almost any responsibility. Surely you have noticed the slump-shoul-dered husband sitting in the passenger seat just looking as though his brain is in shut-down mode. It bothers me that I see so many old men strapped in their seats appearing as though they are in a mindless coma. Come on, guys. At least look around and feign interest in the world around you.

In my case, I am beginning to realize that my wife, Kay, may be a better driver than me. She correctly accuses me of looking around at everything when I drive. Indeed I do. My unflagging curiosity wreaks havoc with my focus. We moved from Virginia to Texas in the mid-eighties and I had to take a driving test to get my Texas driver's license. It should have been a snap, right? Well, I darn near failed it, because the officer testing me told me I spent too much time looking around at everything rather than focusing of my driving. Again, guilty as charged. When Kay drives, driving has her un-divided attention. I have reluctantly turned much of our driving over to her. Damn, it has been very difficult for me to admit she might be a better driver.

On the other hand, I have thoroughly enjoyed the freedom to take in the landscape, farms, cattle, and other sights we pass without it being inter-rupted by having to drive. Every now and then, I even see a mule or a field full of fainting goats. One year Kay and I went to the Deschutes County Fair in Redmond, Oregon. Once I discovered the animal barn had several pens of fainting goats, I quit looking at the rest of the fair. I told Kay that when she had seen it all, come back to the goat pens to pick me up for the ride home. Oh, the sights I have seen.

While this chapter is supposed to be about urges, the bit about Buicks has made me think of some old folks' driving habits that need discussing. I have noticed that lots of us older people get in our exit lane far, far in ad-vance of when it's required. This action harms no one, with the possible ex-ception of the passenger. I wonder if drivers who do this are just frightened by the chance of getting trapped in the wrong lane when it's time to turn. Certainly, when we get older, we question ourselves more than before and we do things—including driving—with less confidence than we once had.

As older drivers, we have all experienced the driver that approaches us from behind at a rate of speed reminiscent of that achieved by a jet just before lift-off. That driver, who is nearly always much younger than we, gets right on our bumper and often accentuates his frustration with our lack of speed by making "what's up" hand signals and "scoot over" hand gestures aimed at conveying his disgust with our driving. His hand signals—some of which are nasty—are usually accompanied by head shakes and frowns. Blinking headlights are also a common means of communicating anger and frustration to an elderly driver who is doing the legal speed limit. Taking driver abuse is just part of life to us older motorists. In fairness, I should tell you I am much calmer about this abuse while writing about it than I am in real life. When an impudent driver starts sharing his thoughts with me about my driving that doesn't match his hurriedness, I usually return the favor. I will even invite these angry road warriors to pull over for a discussion or physical confrontation. I am trying hard to break this in-your-face reaction because so many people now solve their conflicts with guns. I'm too slow to dodge bullets. If a young man and I go face-to-face, I figure I have the advantage. I simply tell the irate fellow that if he whips me, he'll be ridiculed by his friends and the public for beating up a man in his mid-seventies, and, further, that if I whip him, he will be ridiculed by those same friends for having been whipped by a man in his mid-seventies. If he still wants to mix it up, well, I'm game. I'm a big, strong man that can hit like a mule kicks. Also, I have lost fights before and one more loss on my sketchy ledger won't devastate me. I know I'm too old to think like this, but I haven't yet checked out of life. We are who we are.

Before I got sidetracked by my runaway machismo, I meant to sum up my narrative about drivers who hassle us oldies for our slow driving, by re-minding them they really shouldn't want a bunch of senior citizens speeding on the streets and highways of America. Our reflexes are way too slow for us to be able to control a speeding, lane-changing automobile. They should pray we continue to drive slowly and doff their backwards caps to us as they speed around us. They need to think through their anger, grin to themselves about the stupidity of pushing old folks to higher speeds and move on.

While I wouldn't call it an urge, I have found that when old folks gather, the discussion doesn't take long to get around to discussing health issues. I think we enjoy these discussions because they enable us to monitor how we stack-up against other members of our over-the-hill peer group. We don't want our friends to have health problems, but when they do, we take some inner delight that we don't have to deal with that particular problem. For at least a moment, it lets us tell ourselves we must be doing okay for our age since we don't suffer from their ailment. I have a group of friends I work out with at the fitness center. We spend some of our between-reps respites together checking on each other's aches and pains, but we also tell jokes and ask trivia questions about movies, television, sports, and world affairs from our shared pasts. While the health discussions are often downers, the other discussions make us laugh and feel good. Our visits to the fitness center help us to stay physically fit and mentally energized. Time well spent. I highly recommend it. It also needs to be pointed out that many urges go unfulfilled. Case in point; I still have delicious sexual urges.

I really don't know how to end this chapter on urges. I'll do so by saying I want to keep having urges and desires. They are proof that I am still alive and planning on a future. If that closing statement doesn't meet your standards for an exit thought for this chapter entitled "An Old Man's Urges", I will just end it by saying, this old man has the urge to end this chapter.

WHAT'S UP WITH HAIR?

In retrospect, I now realize that Mother Nature eases us into old age, sometimes so subtly that we fail to notice the cumulative effect of her small, minor adjustments to our being. She drops lots of seemingly innocuous warnings of the impending storm about to swamp our lives. For example, the first gray hair that springs up seems kind of cute and harmless. We often even joke about it in a mock-horror way, but we sort of think of it as a badge of honor that signals our arrival at full maturity and hails our ascendency to wisdom. Let's talk about hair and how it relates to our aging.

One's hair acts as though it can't wait to tell the world of our aging. Once it decides to turn gray, it goes nuts and seemingly races to complete the process at break-neck speed. The same thing can be said of the thinning of the hair. When one first notices a receding hairline, a slightly balding spot, or too much hair showing up in his or her hairbrush, that soul would be well-advised to strap in because the mad dash to baldness has begun, and it's a fast and furious charge to the finish line. In some men, the dash to baldness, for some reason, often stops short of accomplishing total bald-ness, opting instead to leave a ring of hair around the lower part of the head. The creation of this Friar Tuck look has led to lots of weird comb-overs and some pretty funky and fakey hairpieces. I suppose barbers and toupee sellers are glad Nature halted the balding process before it was completed.

The appearance of rogue hairs on strange places on the body has been written about ad nauseum for years, but they are an oddity of aging and, as such, cry out for re-mentioning. Rogue hairs, also known as wild hairs, follow no patterns. I found a thin, blonde hair on my belly that had quietly and secretly attained a length of about five inches before I discovered it. I was fascinated by it and refused to cut it, choosing instead to see how long it would become before a washcloth or bath towel uprooted it. It maxed out at around six inches and then went to where dead hairs go. It quickly sprang back out and started its trek back to prominence all over again. That process of grow-drop off-regrow has now repeated itself countless times. What fun! The older I get, the easier I am to entertain.

Another oft-told hair story associated with aging is the one about hairs' late-in-life fascination with growing in nostrils, ears, and the space between the eyebrows. I think the afore-mentioned hair adventures apply al-most exclusively to men. The mere thought of wiry, black hair growing out of a woman's ears is both frightening and a tad bit humorous. Personally, I would struggle mightily to find a hairy-eared woman even remotely sexy or attractive. I am disturbed by even the image of such a woman. When I whisper sweet nothings into the ear of my lady, I don't want my lips to be tickled by bushy ear hair. I'm funny that way. If women feel that way about hairy-eared men, don't tell me. I'm rather fragile.

Once the hair invasion of the ears, nostrils, and the here-to-fore hairless zone between the eyebrows occurs, men have to get their barbers (or stylists) to help with their grooming. I would never ask my barber to trim my nostrils, preferring instead to handle that clumsy chore in the privacy of my own bathroom. My son gave me a battery-operated nose hair trimmer as a gift a few years ago. Understanding the implied meaning of his unusual gift, I use it. I do, however, ask the barber to clip my ear hair and thin my eyebrows. They seem to think nothing of the request, probably because so many older men share this furry malady.

I had an uncle who loved to read. He would often retreat to his family's seldom-used formal living room, plop down in his favorite chair, and lose himself in the pages of a good western novel by Frank Dobie or Zane Grey. As he did so, he became oblivious to the world around him. He was so engrossed by his book, he was seemingly unaware of his habit of yanking nose hair and ear hair as he read. While the yanks were rather violent, they never seemed to deter my uncle from his literary trance. In fairness to my uncle, as an older gentleman, I can now relate to his war on unwanted hair. For those of you who cannot fathom the intricacies of hair removal by yanking, let me tell you that uprooting nose hair from your nostrils is momentarily painful and often tear-inducing. As is often said, aging is not for sissies.

Women. I really know very, very little about how aging affects women's hair. I'm not going to ask either. A walk down that road would be akin to the Bataan Death March. Can you imagine the looks I would get if I asked women to tell me where unwanted hairs have popped-up in their old age? Being a keen observer of human nature has suggested to me that women are considerably touchier about their aging than men are. In this case, propriety has trumped my desire to expand my research. Oh, I've noticed the occasional facial hair on "mature" women, and I know hormonal changes often play havoc with women's hair and other stuff. I, also, know quite a few women fight the thinning hair battle with creams, pills, and hair extensions for much of their lives. I suspect that's about where my knowledge of women's age-related hair challenges is forever stopped. After seeing how many women spend tons of money to alter the color of their hair, I have no expectations of having honest discussions with women about their hair.

Women seem to allow hair—it's color, its style, its thickness, etc.—to dramatically affect their public and self-image. Some men do the same, but not so many. By paying so much attention (and money) to their hair, women have elevated it into becoming a means of attracting the attention of men and other women. Sometimes I am reminded of fancy birds that display their beautiful feathers in hopes of attracting the perfect mate. In the case of birds, however, it is usually the males strutting around showing off their array of feathers, Not so with humans. By not caring that much about the appearance of their hair, men have managed to turn their indifference into a chick repellant. Women and men are just different; very different. Some men color their hair. It seems to me that most of those who do so, do it poorly. For some reason, most bad hair dying efforts look like someone has applied shoe polish to their hair. I'm fully aware of the fact that men who get good hair coloring applications escape detection by those who look for such age-defying maneuvers. Only the bad hair jobs get noticed. Toupees and wigs are like hair-dye jobs. Some are great, while others just don't work.

Before I leave the subject of hair and its effects on aging, let me talk about disappearing hair. I used to have hair on my legs. I never was super-hairy, but I had leg hair. One morning in my late 60s, I woke up, and my leg hair had disappeared. Had the hair fairy stolen it from me in the middle of the night? Had my testosterone gauge hit zero that night and just let my hair leave the building? My wife went through a similar experience when she realized she didn't have to shave her legs anymore. There was no hair. Hairless legs may be a godsend to women, but they toy with a man's concept of his own masculinity. It is possible that some of that AWOL leg hair snuck around my body and took root in my back. I now have back hair! What's up with that? I live in the Arizona desert and shorts are part of the state's official uniform. When folks ask me if I shave my legs, I smile and say "yes." I add that doing so is a requirement spelled out in my contract with Speed-O Swim Wear.

My doctor told me that the loss of leg hair sort of went along with the loss of testosterone. That was not good news, because testosterone is a vital ingredient of our masculinity, and no man wants to think of himself as less masculine than he's always been. During my drive home from the doctor's office, I recalled that as my hair fell off my legs, it started growing in my ears and nose. Does that mean my testosterone is now all in my ear and nose? If so, what the hell does that mean?

End of discussion.

Yes, end of discussion.

THE GREAT SOUTHERN SKIN MIGRATION

I've often thought hair and skin have partnered up into an assault force dedicated to ravaging our bodies, brains, and looks, to announce our old age to the world. It's a conspiracy of two powerful enemies of our youth that, once they marshal their strength and formulate their coordinated attack plan, run over and through our bodies with a ruthlessness matched only by Sherman's devastation of Georgia in the Civil War. Their shared goal is to leave us old and old looking. They form an unholy alliance.

NEWS FLASH!

I hereby recommend that the American Medical Association recognize Southern Skin Migration as a new disease. It attacks everyone somewhere along the trail to old age. There are no known natural cures for it, and it is painful to those who suffer from it. I further propose that the Center for Disease Control and Prevention put a team of expert researchers to work learning more about this devastating disease and finding a cure for it. Shall I put these recommendations in the form of a motion? Can I get a second, or at least an amen? Thank you. And now back to our narrative.

I've witnessed this assault on my face and body with curiosity and even a bit of admiration for the tactical excellence the perpetrators have demonstrated. Somewhere, along my age line, the commander of my skin gave the order for all of my skin to drop its defenses against its march—or fall—southward. The march started slowly, but soon the southward migration began to take its toll. Like a snowball rolling downhill, it seemed to pick-up size, speed, and power as it went along. The Battle of the Sag was underway, and I had no defenses capable of stopping its progress.

Now, even my eyebrows have moved southwardly off of my brow bone where they had homesteaded for years. Is it possible for eyebrows to eventually go below the eyes? I'll let you know in a few years. Conjures up a disturbing image doesn't it? My eyelids drooped down over my eyes so much they impaired my vision. A modified eyelift was necessary to restore my range of vision. The skin on my face seemed to turn loose of its roots and yield its firmness, seemingly taking on the properties of melted candle wax. Now, when shaving, I have to pull on my skin to get it taut enough for the razor to glide over it. Otherwise, my skin will just slide around under the movement of the razor. My neck whiskers have moved south so much they are threatening to leave my neck and arrive on my upper chest. If this trend continues, I will soon have to take off my shirt to shave.

A lot of my facial skin has gathered under my jaw bone and formed into jowls. "Jowls" is an ugly word. Jowls are an even uglier facial feature. I once heard an elderly comedienne comment that her turkey neck was so pronounced she dared not leave the house during the Thanksgiving Holidays. I hear you, dear.

We all know our breasts head south on us as we get older. It is undoubtedly easier to spot this southern flow on women, but men are also affected. If I live long enough, my nipples will end up on a line where my navel used to be and my navel will have nearly reached the South Pole. I now realize I took the firmness of my skin for granted. Now that it has been replaced by elasticity, I miss it. I know lots of people—mostly women—opt for cosmetic surgery in search of firmness for their skin and the relocation and re-sizing of body features. I can't really blame them for trying to hold on to their waning youth or improve their looks. In a moment of honesty, I must tell you I've thought it might be nice to have a total skin lift, but if Medicare won't pay for it, I'll have to pass.

I was told what I presume was a joke about a man who waited patiently for his wife's facelift and breast enhancements to heal enough to be unveiled in a romantical setting. When the night came for the revealing moments, the husband was excited and impressed with his "new" playmate. As fate would have it, that same night, the husband was struck down with his first episode of erectile disfunction. Poor guy.

I don't care for Botox-injected lips, however. One time I was playing golf in Austin and, unbeknownst to me, a yellow jacket had crawled inside my open Dr. Pepper can. When I took a sip of my "pepper upper," the yellow jacket stung my lips several times before I could spit it out. My lips puffed-up something fierce. The pain of the stings went away fairly quickly. The swollen lips hung around through dinner. It was a bad look; a very bad look. Not one soul told me my swollen lips improved my looks. Women with Botox-filled lips look to me like they had a mad yellow jacket in their Dr. Pepper can.

I think women look good with nice hair and some make-up. I suspect nice hair and make-up have kept some marriages together into old age. The bad hair and all-natural look is not kind to every woman, but, for the most part, I really find women in their unenhanced state to be near the peak of their attractiveness. While I admit to editorializing quite a bit about what men and women should and should not do as they battle against the ravages of aging, I'm just offering my opinion. I admire and love lots of folks who fight aging through enhancements. I, also, admire and love lots of folks who haven't gone the enhancement route and are as ugly as home-made soap. I hope they feel the same about unenhanced ugly old men. I remember when people occasionally told me I "looked good." If they do so now, they always add, "for your age." In my own case, I am too curious to see what God has in store for me in the looks department as I age to re-design myself. I can handle ugly. It should be noted here that I have found one of the nicest things about getting old is that good looks has nothing to do with love. It may have something to do with attraction, but love is a whole different kettle of fish as it goes much deeper than surface looks. As elders, we now have the wisdom to discard attaching great value to the unimportant things such as looks, wealth, jewels, and other things that have no eternal value, and focus on the heart, mind, and soul of people. We are now better at putting our love where it belongs. Now, we all know not everyone buys into this revision and discovery of what is ultimately of the greatest value. Some still love their money, their power, and their toys.

I planned on having a chapter about wrinkles in this book, but I couldn't come up with enough material to justify it. Since wrinkles are basically the result of skin falling down on top of other skin or pushing up against it, thus creating a ditch between the two skin folds, wrinkling is hard to stop once the process has begun. We know smoking and sun tanning rush the onset of wrinkles and add to an individual's unattractiveness. Mother Nature can mark a fellow up pretty well without the aid of Marlboros or sunshine. Some folks wrinkle better than others. For example, happy, smiling people get grin lines that can be quite attractive. On the other hand, frown lines tend to paint one as a grouchy, pessimistic, and/or an unhappy person. I'm not declaring those different kinds of wrinkles are true indicators of an individual's personality. I'm just suggesting that wrinkles can suggest personality traits, at least at first glance.

WARNING!

Nothing I say about aging in this book is supported by medical science or geriatric studies. Nothing. These are just my observations and, sometimes, guesses. I may not be qualified to make serious observations or recommendations associated with the aging process, but I am entitled to do so. It's my book, and I am old. And now, back to our narrative.

My mother-in-law, Billie Hightower, died at age 91. Right up to the time of the series of strokes that got the best of her, she lived a life of go, go, go. She was indefatigable and always seeking her next adventure before her current one was over. She was smart, adventurous, and set on action right up until the end. She treated all of her health issues as though she couldn't figure out why she had any problems. In her mind, she was too young and "healthy" for nuisances like high blood pressure, arthritis, high cholesterol, and sundry aches and pains to impinge on her lifestyle. When doctors reminded her that she was at the age when imperfections in one's health began to arise with regularity, she didn't buy it. All of "those" sorts of ailments plagued the elderly—not her. When something went wrong or hurt her, her first reaction was surprise. Her first comment was usually, "Well, I've never had that problem before," suggesting that it had no business messing with her and that it would pass quickly.

In her mid-eighties, her eyesight began to fade. Finally, in her late eighties, she consented to have cataract surgery. All went well until she discovered her new-found vision and looked into the mirror. She was absolutely distraught at what she saw and called each of her three children in a state of near panic. She announced to all that her eye surgeon had obviously botched the cataract procedure and caused her to have big, deep wrinkles in her face that she didn't have prior to the surgery. With tears in her eyes and a trembling voice, she accused the surgeon of having done something like clip a nerve that caused the devastating wrinkles. Finally, after much patient reasoning from her kids, she began to buy their story that the wrinkles had long been there and were not new to her face. Her dramatically improved eyesight simply allowed her to see the wrinkles better than she had ever seen them before. She wasn't happy with the news but professed to believing it. I'm not 100% certain she really did completely absolve the surgeon of malpractice but might have just been placating her kids by saying she bought their story. That incident reminded me that we're seldom happy with what aging does to our looks—even into our nineties.

While I'm on the subject of my beloved mother-in-law, Miss Billie, I have to tell you about her failing taste buds. By the time she was in her late eighties, her taste buds had worn out. She drank lots and lots of incredibly hot black coffee for most of her life, and I theorize she just burned those delicate little taste buds completely up. Regardless of what caused their death, the absence of taste buds became a big problem for Billie and those around her. She conveniently ignored her inability to taste food and accused most of the cooks and chefs of East Texas of being lousy at their jobs. It was obvious to her, they were all incapable of preparing food that tasted good. Her dissatisfaction with the culinary artists of East Texas would have been tolerable to those with whom she was dining if she had just kept her grumbling at the table. She didn't. Billie complained to the helpless waitresses and waiters and raised hell with the restaurant manager or owner about his or her need to hire a new chef. She could be an ornery old gal. Lovable, but ornery. By the way, if a cook in the East Texas I grew up in wanted to be called a chef, he just needed to be able to make at least four kinds of gravy and buy a chef's hat. Just an aside.

A huge industry has sprung up in our world selling anti-aging products and services. Cosmetic surgery, hair thickeners, dyes, shots and pills that make soft things hard, pec and butt implants, breast enlargements, knee and hip replacements, dental implants and, lastly, expensive wrinkle-removing creams. Kay and I gave in to the relentless advertising campaign for a product the manufacturer claimed was a "magical" cream that made wrinkles disappear for hours at a time and ordered this wonder cream on line. We were excited when it arrived and eager to test it out. Kay rubbed some of it under her eyes and could quickly feel the tightening of her skin. We were hopeful and decided it was working. It worked —for fifteen minutes. I'm sure it works longer for some folks, but we maxed out at fifteen minutes. Bummer. Wish I had our $60 back.

As we age, we begin to realize our skin will have its way with us. Efforts to delay its devastation of our youthful looks, i.e. facelifts, implants, magic creams, gobs of make-up, etc., are stop-gap measures that often help for a while and from a distance. However, the reprieve they offer to the aging is fairly short-lived. At some point they might even look silly on an older person. We've all seen faces that have had one too many skin-stretching procedures. The skin looks like a thin, tightly stretched onion skin that looks as though it might pop if bumped into. As I've said before, I don't blame folks for trying to fend off the effects of aging. Sometimes it helps. Sometimes it doesn't. Another way to avoid wrinkles is to get fat. Obesity seems to fill the skin with fat, which leaves no room for wrinkles. Taut skin is wrinkleless and quite attractive.

Since this chapter is devoted to skin, please allow me to issue a suggestion, or perhaps a warning, to young people. If you want to look your best in old age, steer clear of smoking, avoid, or, at least minimize tattoos and suntans.

I started smoking at an early age because I thought it was cool and both of my older brothers were smokers. I tanned every summer because—in all honesty—everyone looked better with a good tan. Tattoos were pretty much taboo throughout society in the days of my youth and were strictly verboten by my parents. If I were a young fellow today,, who's to say whether or not I would ink up. I pretty much went along with the crowd back then and I wasn't particularly worried about what my youthful proclivities would do to my looks or health in my golden years—say past forty.

Subjecting your skin to any or all of these skin-altering actions when you are young may make you temporarily popular with your peers and somewhat more attractive for a while, but know this fact for certain, none of these temporary skin enhancements age well. Smoking does a number on one's face, particularly the eyes, and they stain over the healthy glow of one's skin. Tattoos warp into ugly ink stains on old, droopy skin. They become reminiscent of something colored by a young child who couldn't stay inside the lines. Pray for wisdom before you ink up. Now, in all fairness, if one wants to have someone tattoo a small, cute butterfly or honey bee in a spot not so easily viewable by us critics, enjoy! It's those who get started tattooing themselves and can't stop until large pieces of their bodies are inked over that cause me angst. I remember when those whose bodies were covered in ink, were stars of the side shows at county fairs and carnivals. Skin that has been fried too many times loses its strength and collapses into deep wrinkles and looks like beef jerky. Smoking, over-exposure to the sun, and tattoos galore are aging agents on steroids.

When I was in junior and senior high school, we all tanned. It made us look better and, in fact, made us look healthier than our pale-skinned classmates. At least we thought it did. None of us knew anything about melanoma or how the frying of our skin with sunshine could hasten aging. None of us were warned that killing our skin with sunshine in order to tan up would cause our skin to prematurely wrinkle and surrender our appearance to old age ahead of schedule. I have a friend who was—and may still be—a tanning freak. Her dark tanned skin looked good on her in her 20s and 30s. By the time she hit her mid-forties, her skin started to repay her for all the sunshine she had inflicted on it. She no longer looked so great. By the time she hit 50, her skin looked like she had had a skin graft from an alligator. She had fried away her good looks.

There's a unanimous consensus that smoking is a death-inducing, stinky, obnoxious habit. I did it for more than 40 years, so I feel entitled to speak on the subject with some authority. I'll stave off the urge to lecture everyone on the hazards of smoking, and I will focus my wrath only on the nasty things smoking does to our skin.

Our skin, also, does not escape the effects smoke has on the wrinkling of our skin. Look at a smoker's eyes and you will have no trouble spotting the discoloration of them or the wrinkles and puffiness that surrounds them. If we use our intelligence and assess the downsides of smoking, we will not smoke. Got it? For the sake of your skin, health, and smell, forestall your visible aging by not smoking. Besides, stinking is bad for your sex life.

I lost my dad and both of my older brothers prematurely to smoking. They were my heroes, and I miss them terribly. My brothers tried to quit many times. My oldest brother, Homer, even quit for 12 years, but started back in his early 50s. He said that every morning during those 12 years, he read the newspaper looking for a headline that read, "Doctors Wrong: Smoking Is Good For You." Never happened. Brother Robert decided smoking was worth an early death to him. He halted all efforts to quit by his mid-forties. Robert was a very intelligent man, and he simply decided the pleasure he received from smoking outweighed his desire to live to a ripe old age. As he lay dying from cancer, he could only whisper. It was obvious he had very little time left. I was standing by his bed and, with his eyes, he signaled me to come closer. I bent close to him so I could hear his faint whispers. I was expecting him to utter some dramatic end-of-life wisdom. Instead, he said, "I saw Jesus. Jesus smokes." He gave me a wry smile and drifted off to sleep. Robert always had a slightly perverted sense of humor but, to this day, I don't know if he was just trying to be funny or if he saw Jesus puffing on a Camel. It's possible that Heaven is what we want it to be. Maybe Jesus will have a smoke with Robert.

The health of our skin plays a major role in the speed with which we age. I've ventured off into editorializing a bit, but I'll close by suggesting you conjure up an image of a senior citizen that has smoked and tanned for most of their lives and now sits before you with sagging tattoos pulling on their skin. Pretty yucky, huh? In the final analysis, we can sometimes stave off the devastations of the aging process to our skin for a while. Not for long.

MIRRORS

At my age, I'm not sure how I feel about mirrors. I do know they play inordinately big roles in forming the self-image we carry around with us each day.

As a relatively carefree kid in elementary school, I don't remember having a reliance on mirrors for anything. I seemed to know who I was and didn't need to stare at myself in the mirror for any kind of confirmation or boost of confidence. As best I can recall, the only times I even stood before a mirror were to either practice making funny faces with which to entertain my classmates or to check out how bodacious I looked in my Little League Giants baseball uniform.

When I got to junior high school, I began to pay closer attention to girls, and I felt the urge to look good to them. This desire led to my caring about how my hair looked, how my clothes looked, and which stances and facial expressions were most likely to make me irresistible to girls. When one is concerned with how they look, they start to devote more and more time staring at themselves in mirrors. The search for perfection can be a very time-consuming exercise, even if it is an effort mired in futility. Once puberty settles in and assumes management of a teen's mind and body, mirror popularity soars. Girls even start carrying mirrors in their purses and, before any important event, meeting, or special encounter, they give themselves a last-minute inspection with their mirror in hand.

Once an individual develops a mirror dependency and links the checking of it to their self-confidence, they simply cannot return to the pre-mirror simpler times. They are addicted to using the mirror and use it to polish themselves up for their public appearances for many, many years to come— maybe even forever. Getting old, however, does tend to reduce one's use of mirrors because the feedback it gives us is seldom good news. I read a birthday card that said, "They aren't making mirrors like they used to. The ones I buy now are full of wrinkles."

I generally think mirrors boost our self-esteem throughout our youth and most of our working lives. When we pass our morning mirror review, we usually venture into our school or business day with zip in our walk and a bit of a "bring it on" attitude. In these regards, the mirror is our friend. In fact, we become so mirror-friendly we check ourselves out in any reflection we happen to encounter. Shiny car fenders, reflective windows, polished aluminum, and even other people's reflective sunglass lenses provide the reflection-hungry among us with impromptu mirrors. Viewing oneself on a video chat is a great example of how folks do this espying of their own images today.

I work out three days a week at a local fitness center. It's a very large facility, and its clientele ranges from folks trying to get in shape, to folks trying to lose weight, to people like me, who are trying to stave-off totally surrendering to old age. The center where I work out, is particularly popular with serious body builders who have muscles on top of their muscles. When I'm at the gym with those Schwarzenegger wannabes, I look like the "before" to their "after." Like every fitness center I've been in, this facility has scads of mirrors. I'm told fitness centers feature lots of mirrors because serious fitness and body buildering freaks need mirrors to allow them to check out their form and posture when they exercise or lift. I don't buy it. I think it is a vanity thing, pure and simple. No one can resist sneaking a peak of themselves in a mirror, whether it's in a department store, doctor's office, or a fitness center. That's a human thing. However, reflection gazing is epidemic in my fitness center. I'm really surprised many young hard-bodies don't get serious whiplash from glancing over their muscles and shoulders for ego-nurturing glimpses of their physiques. In a number of cases, I think they would change gyms if the mirrors were removed. In truth, if I had muscles like these mirror addicts, I might fall in love with my image, too. I don't, and I haven't. During my workouts, I do sometimes check myself out in the mirror. I'm not checking out my bulging muscles (I don't have any); I'm reminding myself to hold in my belly. What makes the mirror gazers comical is not that they like staring at themselves. Like I said, that's human. It's that they try to act as though they are not staring at themselves. Own up to your vanity, fellows. We all know what you are doing. Yep, the jig is up.

I reiterate, no one can pass up a chance to look at himself in a mirror. I had been working out for a few months and thought I could tell the difference in the size of my muscles. One night, after a shower, I was feeling pretty body-happy so I stood in front of the mirror and went through a series of muscle-flexing poses. I was just short of calling Kay to come admire the new me when I pulled a muscle in my back. The pain was so intense, I dropped to my knees. I did, in fact, call for Kay to come in, but it wasn't because I wanted her to admire the new me. It was because I needed her help to get up. My beautiful new body had blown a tire. Sometimes, God is less than subtle when He resets our egos. All those hours of working in the gym, and I never injured myself. One minute of flexing in front of my mirror and bam! Show over.

If we follow the normal aging process, our senses and thought processes start losing their acuity the older we get. Eyesight and hearing struggle to keep up. Even if we stand before a well-lit mirror, our eyes often fail to sharply see all that is before them. Because our sight is not what it used to be, we start to make vision-related mistakes. Men have trouble giving themselves a good shave. Quite often, little patches of unshaven whiskers start showing up. Men aren't skipping these whiskery areas on purpose. They just no longer see them. The same sort of problems show up in older women's application of make-up. It often appears their make-up has been applied unevenly. That's because their old-person vision won't let them see well enough to do a good job. As I mentioned earlier, the more a mirror lets us down, the less dependent we become on it.

I am certain you have noticed how addicted younger people are to taking photos of themselves. Selfies, as they are called, are both obsessive and excessive. Cellphones have warped people's sense of what's important and what is useless garbage. Who in the world wants photos of you doing all the things you do when you are just living your life? When people spend so much time taking pictures of themselves and sending them throughout the world via social media such as Facebook, Instagram, and Snapchat, doesn't it seem as though they are wasting the valuable time they have on this earth? It's a scarce commodity, you know. Besides, I really can't imagine there's a large group of "followers" who can't wait for you to post that new photo of you licking an ice cream cone, thrilling though it may be. Come to think of it, I'm shocked people seem to carry their phones around just waiting for that ding that tells them some "important" something has come in on their line. Those waiters are in worse shape than the senders. Just think. Instead of wasting all that time taking selfies—all of which feature that "special" phony smile that appears on your every selfie—you could be doing something that has academic, societal, intellectual, or medical importance, such as writing a book similar to this one (tongue firmly in cheek).

I talked about selfies in this chapter of mirrors because I see them as an extension of our longstanding addiction to mirrors. Any way you cut it, we just love seeing ourselves in mirrors, selfies, snapshots, etc.; at least until we get old. Then, not so much.

Personally, I will take mirrors over cameras any day. I can usually stand in front of a mirror and find something to like about the way I look. If I stand there long enough, I can eventually stare myself handsome, at least a little bit. Also, some mirrors are so poorly lit they don't reflect all of one's imperfections. Now that I think about it, I may dislike bright light more than I dislike mirrors. I absolutely need bright light by which to read, but I don't want it to expose the depth of my wrinkles or the sag of my skin.

Photographs? Well those suckers just won't lie for you, unless you can manipulate them through Photoshop, which very few elderly folks know how to use. In general, a snapshot is a true, accurate reflection of what you look like at that moment in time. One can stare at a photo for hours on end, and it won't change. It's reality, plain and simple. See why I prefer mirrors to photographs? By the way, have you ever seen anyone look good in a police mug shot? The answer is "no". A police mugshot makes everyone look like a hardened criminal. Vlad the Impaler must have trained all of the police photographers in the world.

Body reflections, in general, are seldom kind to the elderly. I'm not certain of all the things that combine to remodel our physiques in old age. Clearly, it's an unholy alliance of factors and influences like hormones, testosterone, physical inactivity, poor diet, television, and a general lack of discipline that chases youth out of our bodies. On the holy side, God just starts the unwinding process in us. When those factors claim control of our bodies, it's as though we've checked into a novice sculptor's studio and gave him the right to reshape us as he pleases. We ultimately walk out of that studio looking the way a poorly trained sculptor would have us look. It is very seldom a good look. The finished product in men usually has a paunch pushing on his belt buckle, a loss of muscle definition, sagging skin, a butt that lost its shape, and an energy level that matches his new body.

I realize I'm on thin ice when I try to describe the re-make a woman's body goes through when old age takes the helm. However, there's little they can do to punish me at my age, so I will give it a shot. I mentioned above that men lose their butts in this aging process. I now think their butts just migrate to women and attach themselves to the derrieres of the fairer sex. In other words, men's butts get smaller while women's butts get larger. Like men's, women's sag factor runs amok. There's lot of sag in old age. Women are also prone to pot bellies in old age. For some reason, spare fat seems to enjoy hanging beneath a woman's bicep. Little kids love to jiggle this stuff and can entertain themselves endlessly by doing so. Who said getting old can't be fun?

Quite a few men get big protruding bellies that cause unforeseen problems. For example, if a man has a big belly, he has a terrible time deciding where to cinch-up his belt. If he straps it around his round belly, it won't stay there. It either slips above the belly, making him look a bit cartoonish, or it slips below the belly, making him look like a beer-swilling bubba. I don't know if women have this problem or not. I have a pretty big belly myself. It's not fair to call it a beer belly. It, more accurately, should be referred to as a chicken fried steak belly.

As noted earlier, I work hard in the gym to try to fight losing complete control of my body. As mentioned above, I still have a protruding belly I just can't get rid of. I think my problem is that physical exercise makes me very, very hungry, so I come home from the gym and head straight for the refrigerator. I then pig out and, for the most part, graze continuously until bed time. The harder I work out, the more I eat. Oh my, what to do?

Make no mistake about it, I hate—or, more accurately, hated—losing my youthful look, but I understand why it happened and I'm not depressed by it. My youthful look wasn't all that great, so I didn't lose a whole lot. On the other hand, someone who looked great in their youth probably resents the changes they've gone through more than us average Joes. Most of us have done enough during our productive years to deserve a rest. It's fun to pass the mantle of responsibility to the younger lions. When I say we deserve a rest, I should add we deserve the right to move on to other activities. One of the nice things about getting old is selective memory. In my memory, I was more handsome, more suave, a better athlete, and smarter than I probably was in real life. I wish I could have been the me I now claim I was. Think about it.

When my wife read this chapter, she concluded that reading it would either amuse the reader or depress them, depending upon their mood at the time. I hope you were in a good, jovial mood when you read it. I certainly don't want to depress anyone about getting old. Worrying about it won't stop the aging process. In fact, rumor has it that worrying causes more wrinkles. Let's remember, aging is better for us than dying young. At least I still think so.

Since this chapter is about mirrors, I should probably close it by talking about mirrors. I think mirrors offer reflections of us that we are free to interpret as we choose. If we gaze into a mirror determined to find our faults, we will. If we want to see ugly, we will. If we want to see tired and worn out, we will. If we want to see pathetic and helpless, we will. The flip side of that coin is that if we want to see attractive, we will. If we want to see energy and enthusiasm, we will. If we want to see strength, determination, and independence, we will. We are all well-advised to take optimism, thankfulness, and happiness with us on our next trip to the mirror.

THE FIGHT OR FLIGHT SYNDROME

If you are a tad bit hardheaded and a little bit vain, you might want to go down swinging against aging. You know you can't turn back the clock, but you are damned well convinced you can delay the havoc to which it will subject your body and mind. Lace 'em up, Rocky, because you will have a fight on your hands. You can only hope old age doesn't put you on the canvas in the early rounds.

Age fighters are the folks who stretch out their wrinkles with facelifts, buy "miracle" skin tightening salves, rely on the magic of make-up, color their hair, and dress like they are younger than they are. I don't blame these folks at all. It's their call to "hang on" to their youth as long as possible. I do, however, caution them to use some common sense and not go bananas in their search for the fountain of youth. Those who go too far in their retro race look silly and make good fodder for the gossipers among us. I hate the look of one who has had one too many facelifts. Their skin is so thin and tight, it becomes almost translucent and looks like it would burst open if a fly lit on it. By the way, this paragraph applies to men as well as women.

Knowing that a lot of us seniors take anti-aging supplements, I did a bit of research trying to find which, if any, supplements may actually help slow the aging process. The website healthline.com listed what they believe to be the twelve best anti-aging drugs and supplements.(8) They are:

- Curcumin—the main compound in turmeric and a potent antioxidant;
- Epigallocatechin gallate (EGCG)—found mainly in green tea;
- Collagen—helps prevent skin aging;
- CoQ10—antioxidant that protects against cellular damage;
- Nicotinamide riboside (NR)—helps energy metabolism and DNA repair;
- Crocin—found in Saffron and reduces inflammation and protects against mental decline;
- Theanine—in green tea and fights mental decline;
- Rho Diola—powerful anti-inflammatory;
- Garlic—strong anti-inflammatory with antioxidant properties (9) (also keeps vampires at bay);
- Astragalus—stress reducing herb and promotes immune function;
- Fisetin—therapeutic compound that can kill senescent cells; and,

- Resveratrol—in grapes, berries, peanuts, and red wine—activates certain genes called sirtuins.

If you can pronounce and understand these age fighting supplements, you are not suffering from mental decline. After reading all of the good things about these herbs, spices, and compounds, I wanted to start taking them all. However, I decided I was too late to start fending off old age and, secondly, I couldn't afford all of them. Saffron, which has a lot of Crocin in it, is the most expensive spice in the world. I don't know how much it costs, but I do know you won't be getting any of it from me this Christmas. I believe some supplements are helpful in the effort to slow down aging. I'm just not certain which ones.

The *Scientific Journal of Biogerontology* defines aging as, "The progressive failing ability of the body's own intrinsic and genetic powers to defend, maintain, and repair itself in order to keep working efficiently." Common sense dictates if we can do something to help our bodies to "defend, maintain, and repair themselves," we should. Medicines and supplements make sense when put in this light. Of course, physicians should be our advisors, not *Redbook*.

Exercise shows up on every list of things we can do to slow down the speed of aging. According to Dr. Alex Leif of the Harvard Medical School, "Exercise is the closest thing we have to an anti-aging pill. Not exercising has the equivalent impact on your health as smoking a pack and a half of cigarettes a day." Let that soak in, couch potatoes.

Most of the above prose and comments are focused on the "fight" part of this chapter. If we are tired of fighting our aging, or if we're too lazy to fight, we are into the "flight" phase of aging. Most of us aren't eager to die but like Doris Day sang in her song, "Que Sera, Sera," or what will be, will be. In other words, we will hope for the best but will accept the worst. It's our choice and once we've made it, we live or die with it. If we have quit fighting our aging, we can enjoy certain freedoms we didn't have when we fought against getting old. For one thing, we can eat what we want. The Long Island Weight Loss Institute published a list entitled, "What Foods Speed Up the Aging Process."(9) Here's their list:

- Fries;
- White bread;
- White sugar;
- Margarine;
- Processed meats;

- Dairy;
- Caffeine plus sugar; and,
- Alcohol.

Of course, most of us enjoy every one of those no-no's with the possible exception of margarine. Thank the Lord pizza, chicken fried steaks, eggs, and Mexican food weren't on that list.

There are some rather obvious differences in how old women and old men handle being old. These differences are not always applicable, but I am comfortable offering them up in general terms. When women get old, most of them have rounded off their hard edges and morphed into sweetness. The term "sweet old lady" applies to the majority of them. They are somewhat passive and go out of their way to avoid conflict. Of course, some are still argumentative, selfish, grumpy, and prone to sudden mood swings. Yes, there are still some "old biddies" around, but not too many. Husbands probably have a lot to do with how sweet or grumpy their wives are, and vice versa. Also, grumpy old women were likely grumpy young women.

Old men, on the other hand, can often be described as cantankerous, grumpy, combative, disagreeable, or competitive. In a similar vein to grumpy old women, grumpy old men were probably grumpy young men. Some men mellow out as they age, sometimes reflecting their happiness with giving their competitive juices a rest. However, I suspect the most mellow among us men were pretty mellow and easy going most of their lives. Why do most road rage incidents involve men? Why are most fights between men? Why are most murders committed by men? Why do male gorillas pound their chests? Why do male birds strut around with the chests puffed out and tail feathers fanned? It's all just men being men because they have always felt as though they had to prove their manhood. Now, as women have entered the "rat race" full bore, they, too, have quickly honed their competitive skills and many now go head-to-head with men on many competitive fronts. Things change, huh?

I think the aggressiveness and competitiveness we often see in men—even old men—is primal in nature. We have been competing with each other since pre-historic times. Cave drawings show men clubbing or spearing other men. The pressure was on man to kill the stag before his neighbor could. He had to claim the best cave before the guy in the valley did. He had to be strong enough to protect his wife from the horny neighbor, and his family from the saber-toothed tiger. Those challenges add up to a whole lot of pressure.

Until recently, men faced constant competition for job success and promotions from other men. Competitiveness and aggression have marked men as real men most of their lives and their histories. Those characteristics did not just fade away as we crafted a more civilized and gentler society. Because we have moved from the ages where physical strength was emphasized to an age that calls for more mental toughness and acumen, the competitiveness and aggression may well be bred out of men in the future. Not yet, but in the future. On the other side of the coin, women may well join the competitive and aggressive sides of the ledger as they compete in what used to be a man's world. Things change, and that is an undeniable part of aging.

Whether we choose to fight against the aging process or just sit down and let it happen, there are things we can do to eliminate some of the more disagreeable aspects of aging that often annoy our families and younger associates. Here's my list:

- Freshen the smell of your house. The houses of some old folks smell like an old barn full of cobwebs;
- Gargle—our breaths can easily smell old, too;
- Without going overboard, stay fashionable;
- Move beyond the old hairdo—men and women, but especially women;
- Stay up on current affairs;
- Read; not just Reader's Digest or Redbook;
- Socialize with someone;
- Exercise—puts color in your face, zip in your walk, and distributes the blood throughout your body;
- Be flexible in your thinking—even when you "know" the other person is wrong; and,
- have your money and coupons in order in the grocery check-out line.

Aging is confusing. Remember back to your teen years. They were confusing, too, weren't they? Every stage of life has been confusing to me, even when I was pretty certain I was the smartest person in the world. In truth, old age has probably been the least confusing of all of the times in which I have lived. I have few decisions to make. I have fewer pressures to handle. I've accepted that I am no more than average and I can handle it. I sometimes waver in deciding whether to fight or take flight. You know who I think may worry the most about fighting off aging? I think beautiful, young trophy wives worry the most. The fear of being traded in for a newer model must drive them bonkers.

Whether you decide to fight or let aging take flight makes no difference in the final chapter. I am happy and I hope you are, too.

SETTLING AND EATING

The word "settle" has more than one meaning. When you hear that a dispute has been settled, you know the dispute is over. When you hear some family settled in Iowa, you think of them sinking their roots in a place that is new to them. Sometimes you hear about a young lady settling for some guy beneath what she could have married if she had just been more patient. Now, when you hear the old saying, such-and-such has "settled into old age," it can be interpreted several different ways.

When one is said to have settled into old age, it could mean that he or she has admitted defeat and just given in to old age. The implication is that he has essentially stopped doing and started sitting, as though just waiting for his end time. Interpreting "settle" that way often evokes sympathy for the settler. We are saddened by the fear that this person has stopped finding joy in his life and has lost all of his ambition to actively engage in life during his remaining years. I most commonly see this kind of "settling" in those who have lost their lifelong mate, children, or closest friends. It's as though grief has taken too much of the love, fun, and enthusiasm from this poor soul and left him to be a mere shadow of his former self. When we know people like this who have "settled" into a deep, dark abyss, all we can do is be a friend to them. We can remind them they are still important to someone and offer them opportunities to rejoin life.

Ultimately, aging makes it absolutely necessary for us to settle into new lifestyles. Those new lifestyles can be great and exhilarating, but they definitely will be different than the ones we enjoyed in our younger years. Even though we may feel terrific, we, generally will not have our energy tank registering "full." The loss of much of our speed, agility, and quick-mindedness will put us in the minor leagues of many of the activities we once enjoyed. Hopefully, we won't be out of the game, we will simply be playing with reduced efficiencies and expectations. In my case, if a television show comes on after ten PM, I won't see it. Late night television just doesn't fit my new lifestyle. I now go to bed no later than ten, read for half an hour, and fall asleep. While I was writing this paragraph, a great line popped in my head. Here it is: When I was younger, I would often go to bed and "kink" out. Now, I go to bed and "conk" out.

My new lifestyle is tailor-made for my new capabilities and interests. I spend more time just thinking, probably because it now takes me longer to think through things than it once did. I reflect more, probably because I see much more in my rearview mirror than I do looking forward. I sit more, probably because I now have fewer places to go or things to do. I love more, probably because I now recognize the futility of hating. You get the picture. Age mandates the need for new lifestyles, but remember, those new lifestyles can be glorious. They may be "settling," but in a good way.

In my golden years, I have pretty much "settled" in on my preferences. Oh, my list of preferences is quasi-dynamic in that I add new discoveries to it and erase things of which I've tired. Here are some of the items I've settled on as my preferences:

- my own pillow;
- my favorite coffee mug;
- my own toilet seat;
- my Ultra Double Ply Cottonelle toilet tissue;
- comfortable shoes, regardless of what they look like;
- my television-watching easy chair; and,
- spending my evening with Kay in our own house.

When I say I have "settled" into a fondness for the above-listed items, I am using "settled" as in settling into my comfort zones. These items make me feel warm, fuzzy, and safe. Feeling warm, fuzzy, and safe is comforting to all people, but to older folks in particular. Familiarity and a nice routine take on added importance during our senior years. I used to drive to work different ways each day, fighting the tendency to get into a rut or routine. Now, I seldom go exploring when driving, preferring, instead, to stick to the script. I simply don't want the challenge anymore.

Settling for old inactive people can—and usually does—mean everything you eat or drink "settles" around your mid-section or butt. I have combined "settling" and "eating" in this chapter for no other reason than because my thoughts on each subject are too few to justify stand-alone chapters. I've offered my thoughts on settling so, now, let's talk about food from this old man's perspective.

Why do some folks eat steak tartare, raw fish (sashimi), or raw eggs? Don't the people who eat these foods raw know that fire has been invented? I've had all three of these uncooked foods, but I've only had them once.

In my previous business life, I spent considerable time in Japan and other Far Eastern locales. My hosts often honored me by serving their traditional foods at our dinners. Knowing that my refusal to partake in the eating of their delicacies would be perceived as an insult, I ate some really weird and unenjoyable stuff. I ate fish heads, jellied eels, pigeon eggs, strange sushi, and raw fish. In the name of diplomacy, I had lots of bellyaches and bouts with diarrhea. You should also know I traveled with several bottles of Pepto Bismol.

I cannot remember if we were in Taipei, Taiwan, or Tokyo, but I was seated next to Lynda Bird Johnson Robb at a very formal dinner. She and her husband, Chuck Robb, who was the Governor of Virginia at the time, were the guests of honor. I was Virginia's director of economic development at the time so I frequently traveled with the Robbs. Back to the story of the dinner. Our hosts served Lynda Byrd's entrée with a large fish head on her plate as a token of their esteem. Lynda whispered her disgust to me at having fish eyes staring at her and sneakily transferred the fish head from her plate to mine. Knowing her rejection of the honor would hurt feelings, I gave her a stern look and put the fish head back on her plate. I whispered for her to just grin and bear it. A few minutes later, I felt something plop down in my lap under the table. I quietly retrieved what turned out to be the traveling fish head from my lap. I gave a Lynda my version of a mean look which prompted her to lean over and whisper in my ear, "You grin and bear it." I wrapped the fish head up in my napkin and kept it in my lap until dinner was over. I then put it back on her plate as we were all leaving the table. I doubt our little game of pass-the-fish-head fooled our hosts at all.

As I think about food, I am reminded of how much we take for granted when we are young and healthy. I spent most of my life thinking I would go through life eating any and all things I desired. I didn't spend one minute thinking that someday I would have to go cold turkey on quitting eating many, many of my favorite foods. High cholesterol that led to bypass surgery and type 2 diabetes combined to remove many—if not most—of my favorites from my allowable menu. Maybe the chart below will help make my point:

FOODS I ONCE CHERISHED, BUT CANNOT (OR SHOULDN'T) EAT ANYMORE

NOW TABOO	MY SUBSTITUTE
ice cream	yogurt
creamed potatoes	mashed cauliflower
lemon pie	sugarless cookies
fried meats	baked or grilled meats
butter	low-fat margarine
white bread	multi grain or Keto bread (i.e., cardboard)
French fries	carrot sticks
gravies	dry foods
candy	sugarless "sweets"
chili dogs	chili dogs without the bun
donuts	wheat bagels
shrimp	fresh fish
biscuits	haven't found substitute
pasta	haven't found substitute

It is my strong opinion that not one of the items listed on the "substitute" side of the ledger comes close to measuring up to the food it is intended to replace. If I were on death row (heaven forbid!) and was told to order my last meal, I would order everything that appears on my "taboo" list. Eating every item on that list in one setting may cause me to explode, but at least I would die with a mouth full of happy taste buds.

Most elderly folks love cafeterias. They do so because cafeterias are relatively inexpensive if one chooses his foods moderately. Personally, old age has not diminished my huge appetite. Therefore, when passing down a cafeteria or buffet line, I tend to overpack my plate causing me to run up quite a tab. Cafeterias, also, have enough food choices to allow us to select items that are compatible with our health-oriented diets, and they offer the bland foods that our worn-out digestive systems will tolerate. Those are the principal reasons old folks flock to cafeterias when they can find one. Those reasons are also contributing factors to why cafeterias are not popular with younger and healthier people and have almost disappeared from the dining landscape. As a younger man, I remember getting a case of the heebie-jeebies every time I entered a cafeteria. I was spooked and depressed by the age of the patrons and the smells of the place. I kind of felt as though I had mistakenly chosen to eat from the trough where the old and worn-out folks came to feed. Even the music piped into most of the cafeterias sounded like funeral dirges. Obviously, I have discarded any reservations I may have had about eating in cafeterias at this point in my life. Now, I just wish I could find a good cafeteria.

As I wrap-up this chapter on settling and eating, I'm reminded that regardless of where we are in the aging process, we are constantly required to make age-appropriate adjustments. We had to adjust to school, to puberty, to adulthood, to jobs, to marriage, to parenthood, to retirement, and now, to old age. The fact that we are in a "gearing down" mode does not make us special. It only means we are still alive and making the adjustments we need to make in order to stay alive. It does seem as though old age requires us to spend considerably more time and money trying to figure out what changes or adjustments are required of us. I remember an old saying that advised, "It is not enough to do our best. Sometimes we have to do what is required." I think I'm in that period of life that commands me to do what is required. I don't have time to experiment with options or to just try harder. I can handle that. Having to make adjustments snaps us out of boring routines. Now, I think I'll "settle" into my easy chair and watch a heart pounding round of golf on the Golf Channel while munching on some carrot sticks (yuck).

It's pretty common for me to park in front on the television and munch. I eat most of my meals while watching my favorite programs. It has become obvious to my family that I pay way more attention to the show I'm watching than I do to the eating process. That lack of attention results in food falling from my fork or spoon onto my shirt. The food-to-shirt bit happens often, very often. More often than not, I end up eating and then taking the stained shirt right to the washroom for a liberal dash of Spray 'N Wash. In my book, Spray 'N Wash is a miracle product.

Do I wish I could return to eating an unrestricted diet? Oh, yes and amen. Truth is, if I want to keep living, I have to adjust—or settle—for a diet that has had all of its flavor drained from it. I can handle it though, because I like living a heck of a lot more than I do chocolate ice cream.

HEALTH ISSUES FOR THE AGING

No matter where we fall on the aging scale, we face health issues . As youngsters, we battle diseases like measles, mumps, chicken pox, croup, pink eye, and roseola. Other maladies such as constipation, cuts, scrapes, insect stings and bites, snotty noses, belly aches, earaches, chigger bites, various fevers, and poison ivy are frequent visitors that shadow us into our teen years. Of course, some (too many) children deal with major diseases and health issues that are far too numerous to mention. They are, also, too sad to talk about.

As teenagers, many of our health "challenges" turn from the physical to the mental. Puberty, pimples, and bodily changes are among the numerous scavengers that pick away at our confidence and fragile self-concepts. Rampaging hormones and testosterone keep us addled and off-balance. We don't particularly like what we see when we look in the mirror and we are pretty sure our flaws are visible to everyone in 3D and living color. Oh, we still have our share of physical issues to deal with as teens, but it's the mental infirmities that pose the biggest threats to our smooth sailing. With the help of God, loving parents, and patient doctors, we manage to ease into adulthood where new illnesses, phobias, and mental conditions lurk, just waiting to show us what they have in store for us.

As young adults, we begin to individualize our health profiles. If we go the athletic route, we must learn to deal with sprains, muscle pulls, heat rashes, and occasional fungi. Aspiring entrepreneurs and capitalists often suffer with cases of the "wants" that, left unfulfilled, can turn into the "gotta haves." During this accumulation phase of our lives, we often stretch our finances to the point of breaking. Some of these success chasers will later admit that much of their drive was inspired by wanting to impress their classmates at their ten-year class reunion. In the really old days, folks called this phenomenon "trying to keep up with the Joneses." Flashy cars, club memberships, high-fashion clothes, and expensive haircuts are often the badges worn by these go-getters, and they want everyone to take note of them. There is, also, an innate desire for us to try to prove to ourselves that we can "make it" in the tough old world.

The health issues these young adults face are about the same as those in their age group that aren't particularly concerned with wealth accumulation or financial success with one notable exception. The achievers sometimes suffer from a rare form of encephalitis commonly referred to as the "big head." Now, to be fair, many of those who don't get caught up in the rat race simply don't have the brainpower, the drive, or the competitive juices necessary for success. It should also be noted that many of these over-achievers are fired-up by a powerful desire to prove themselves to themselves. I really can understand that motivation. We need those high-energy go getters in our world, if for no other reason than we need someone to pick up the slack us underachievers have left in our wake. Also, they usually end up hiring those of us who kind of coast through life.

I was born in 1946. At that time, a man's life expectancy was 64.4 years and a woman's was 69.4 years. Women have always had longer life expectancies. In 1990, men lived to 71.8 years and women to age 78.8. We seem to be living longer and longer, but women remain better at achieving old age that us men.

I don't know which agency published this list first, but the Center for Disease Control and Prevention, the NCHS, the American Heart Association, and the Washington State Health Care Authority reported that in 2020, the eight greatest causes of death in America were (10):

1. heart disease;
2. cancer;
3. COVID-19;
4. accidents;
5. respiratory diseases;
6. stroke;
7. Alzheimer's; and,
8. diabetes.

At that same time, extensive surveys showed that old people feared Alzheimer's more than the other fatal diseases combined. Cancer and heart disease round out the top three fears. Old folks realize that if they get Alzheimer's, they will be a burden to their loved ones and caregivers and that is something they do not want to be. They have, also, usually seen the heart-wrenching way most Alzheimer patients die. I think most old-timers fantasize about dying quickly when they go—fast and clean. We should all be so lucky.

While it's hard to pin down the major factors that lead to death, there is consensus that smoking, bad diet (including obesity), alcohol, and harmful drugs speed our race toward death. Aging itself makes us more prone to health problems and is a bit reminiscent of a slow death march. Our objective should always be to maximize the joy we can wring from the entire process. Aging well is a worthy objective. When I am around other senior citizens, I notice that some of them wear frowns that tell me they are either unhappy, angry, or sick. I worry about them, and often pray for their well-being. I also notice those who wear smiles and radiate happiness. They are delightful, and they infect entire gatherings with joy. I am sometimes even moved to ask these happy jacks why they are so happy. I work out at a fitness center with a lady, Lisa, who is in her late fifties, and all of the people in the gym have noticed that she is the epitome of unbridled joy. One day I introduced myself to her and asked her why she was always so upbeat and cheerful. She told me she had Jesus Christ in her life. Thank you, Lisa, for the smile you wear and the joy you spread. I wish I were more like Lisa, and I thank her for reminding me that a walk through life with Jesus Christ at your side enriches that stroll immensely.

As I have aged, surgical procedures have removed countless cysts, warts, and moles from me. My wisdom teeth and a couple of other bad teeth have been pulled. A gifted surgeon shaved off some of the frayed tissue on my rotator cuff. I lost my tonsils and adenoids when I was twenty-five. My hemorrhoids have been excised. Floating pieces of cartilage were removed from my left knee. Four of my cholesterol-clogged heart vessels have been replaced by new ones and I recently had a heart ablation where they went into my heart and zapped a tiny part of it that was misfiring the electrical impulse it was sending out. Much of my prostate gland has been taken out, and my cataracts are a thing of the past. Last year, my surgeon removed a cancerous tumor from my bladder. I guess if one added up all the moles and cysts I've had excised from my body and put them in a pile, it would be quite impressive.

I feel as though God is taking me back on the installment plan. The older I get, the more I have to go in for repairs. I've begun to think of myself as I once did my 1955 Ford. Every time it got to running smoothly, something would go wrong and I would have to take it into Dick Cole at Rayford's Garage for repairs. I feel confident that hip replacements and maybe knee replacements will soon be in order. God is not through harvesting my body parts. Aging is a riot.

My needs have changed over the years. Two things I used to take for granted have emerged as keys to me having a good day. A good night's sleep and enjoying a good bowel movement make my day a whole lot better than it would be without them. I no longer take either for granted. Some of these changes that come with aging lead to concessions in our lifestyles. I have now conceded the following, to name a few things:

• speed of movement;
• quickness of mind and body;
• driving at night;
• eating without spilling;
• complete control of my farts;
• maintaining focus;
• remembering where I left my phone, car keys, or glasses; and,
• the energy to exercise initiative.

I recently ran across the word "feckless" in an article I was reading and had to look up its meaning. It means inefficient and lacking initiative. That definition hit home when applied to me and my age. I'm just plain running low on feck.

My personal deficiencies have led to dependence on helpful devices like:

• glasses;
• hearing aids;
• needles for insulin injections;
• eye drops for dry eyes;
• a C-PAP machine that keeps me breathing while I sleep; and,
• a wide array of miracle drugs that keep me chugging along.

All of those listed items help us immensely. Canes, walkers, and wheel chairs keep a lot of seniors from falling flat on their faces. Pads, diapers, bandages, and braces come in handy for many. No doubt, medicines extend our lives. Have you noticed you now need a bigger medicine cabinet than you did a few years ago? I have. A walk though my house reveals that I have a shoe box full of medicines, a bathroom cabinet full of medicines, a night stand crowded with pills, drops, and sprays, a few odd meds scattered around in unusual places such as the refrigerator. Speaking of medicines, I've become very good at removing childproof caps. I now use a hammer to do so. I read a tongue-in-cheek article that said if you live long enough, the names in your little black book will all start with "Dr." I take three prescriptions, a fish oil supplement, plus a daily baby aspirin, for heart related problems. I take four prescribed drugs for my diabetes, plus a supplement that promises to rid me of the disease all by itself. I take two drugs for dry eyes and three supplements to help them along. I take a pill to keep me in a good mood and one for reflux. Lastly, I throw in a daily multi-vitamin. When all of those pills are added together, I take 11 prescriptions every day plus seven supplements. That's a lot, huh?

Have you noticed that all of the printed material about your medicines is written so small it is darn near impossible to read? I have, but I do normally grab the magnifying glass and read the possible side effects each pill might cause. Some of the more common possible side effects they warn against include dizziness, diarrhea, blindness, erectile disfunction, nausea, depression, muscle aches, itchiness, and possibly death. Oh, you might ask, is that all? If you add all of those possible problems together, you've got…drumroll, please…old age. One of these days, I am going to find a pill with possible side effects that include improved vision, clarity of thought, renewed energy, the disappearance of age spots, the darkening of hair, and a blue steel stiffie. If such a medicine is out there, I guarantee you it's totally illegal.

Here are a few things I wish someone would invent to sell to us old men:

- toe nail clippers that can cut inch thick nails and come with a magnifying glass on the end;
- zipper grease that will speed the process of unzipping for those ever-increasing moments when the need to "go" is urgent;
- a third ear for the back of our head so we can hear our own farts;
- a third eye for the back of our head so we can see if anyone is behind us before we cut loose;
- men's shoes that come with imitation water spots on their toes to help disguise the real ones that often fall on one's shoes in the post-urination process;
- an effective, non-visible girdle that holds in pot bellies, while allowing free breathing;
- brown underwear, and,
- shirts that eat the food we spill on them when we sit on the sofa and munch.

Health for seniors changes daily. Each morning as a senior wakes up he or she does a quick inventory to determine what, if anything, hurts or aches that day. During the day, most seniors are careful to make certain they take their medicines at the prescribed times. We generally equate taking our meds with staying alive. I am truly happy that most medicines are taken orally and are not suppositories. For the most part, we trust our doctors explicitly. We really have no choice but to do so. By the way, do you know what they call the guy that finished last in his medical school class? They call him "Doctor." My dad once told me that the average doctor is only as good at his job as the average plumber is at his. Hmm. Humans are tough and rather resilient. Even those with major health challenges seem to deal pretty well with the rotten hand life has dealt them. You seldom get to old age if you are a wuss.

There are other factors that negatively affect the lifestyles, states of mind, and health of old people. A few of those are: guilt; loneliness; and depression.

For some reason, the older we get, the more we think about the past. I suspect we are in the phase of life when we regularly critique the life we have lived. It's a self-imposed audit. Any critique of ourselves will cause us to regret the things we did wrong in life, the negative effects our personalities and preferences may have had on our loved ones and friends, the bad decisions we made, and the opportunities we missed to be better and to help others. We, inevitably, focus more on our shortcomings than our successes and good points. The above-described process often leads to guilt. About the only antidote for this guilty feeling is for loved ones and friends to remind the elderly of the good they have done and how much they have meant to others in their lives. These kindnesses are truly manna for the souls of the elderly. By the way, asking God to forgive you for your past wrongdoings and oversights is the quickest and surest way to get rid of guilt. Don't forget, however, that for that process to work, you have to forgive those who you think have wronged you.

Loneliness is a real downer. It is, also, a real killer. Loneliness comes from a lack of attention from loved ones and friends. It's exacerbated by the lack of interaction with other people. Who among us has not visited a nursing home and seen a group of the residents in wheelchairs lined up in a row? There's little or no interaction among the group, and the people often have blank stares and appear to be sad. The scene is both depressing and even a little disarming. We really don't know how to act in such a situation.

Clearly these people are lonely and in need of attention. They emit a disturbing aura. Others in care centers spend most of their days in their beds just hoping, I suspect, for a visitor. The image of old people being warehoused waiting to die is unavoidable. Most of these residents have people who love them, but they are too caught up in living their lives to spend adequate time with their older loved ones. No doubt, life is short of time. Too often old folks pay the price for a world that is just too busy.

For many elders, loneliness comes in a huge wave when a spouse of many years passes away. The void, too often, just cannot be filled. The surviving mate soon realizes it's no fun dining alone, shopping alone, traveling alone, or really doing anything alone. There's no longer anyone to share things with or ask questions. Even watching television loses something when done alone. The void left when a much-loved spouse dies just can't be filled. Caring family and friends can help, but they simply cannot replace a spouse. It helps to have someone to cry to and with. After all, tears expunge grief and tragedy from the body. The government of Great Britain recognized the debilitating effects of loneliness a few years ago and created a Department on Loneliness, charged with assisting the elderly who were in the throes of loneliness.

Guilt and loneliness feed the beast of depression. Depression is a monster that can disable a body and cause the depressed to slide into an emotional abyss from which one cannot be easily saved. No one bounces back from depression on their own. The afflicted must be coached, coaxed, and loved back to normalcy. This process normally needs the help of a medical specialist and the patience of loved ones.

While the elderly deal with diseases and worn-out body parts, they, also, have to fight off emotional and mental assaults. It's very tough on one who outlives his or her confidence. Us oldies know we can't stave off death, but we need the help of loved ones and friends as we struggle for survival and fight against depression and flagging confidence. We do not want to be forgotten.

ADJUSTED DESIRES, EXPECTATIONS, AND ASSUMPTIONS

It doesn't take an Einstein or a Dr. Phil to realize our desires and expectations change significantly as we age. Plus, many of the assumptions we have had about aging get corrected along the way.

As a working adult, I wanted to succeed, and success was measured in dollars, power, and the respect of peers. To excel in amassing any one of those three items marked one as successful. To do well in two or three of those categories made one wildly successful. I did okay, but I'll never be in anyone's hall of fame. I'm fine with that because, as we age, we realize there are other kinds of success that take on more significance later in life. Don't get me wrong, I still wish I had achieved higher marks in wealth, power, and success. The ego trip would have been fun. To act as though I am now wise enough to know success in those three areas is meaningless, and in the final analysis, the act would be disingenuous. I think we older folks sometimes act as though those standard measures of success are frivolous as a way of coping with our failure to rise to the top.

Now, let me point out some of the other ways to succeed in life. This list is totally subjective and far from complete. Being successful in achieving excellence in any of these areas is quietly appreciated and acknowledged by mankind, not just a few men and women. Here we go:

- being part of a loving, caring family;
- being loyal to your principles;
- staying out of prison;
- sharing with those who need help;
- bringing light into dark places;
- listening;
- showing gratitude; and,
- telling those you love that you love them.

As a Christian, I strive to succeed in the above-mentioned areas. "Strive" is the key word. I certainly don't have it down pat. Just trying. Whether one is religious or not, those living a life with these elements of love, care, and behavior in their lives are good for our world and successful where it counts. Their successes tend to have greater value than wealth, power, and fame. Now, pass the offering plate, brother.

I remember my ten-year high school reunion. We all strutted around like peacocks trying our hardest to look suave and successful. I even bought a new yellow sport coat for the event. I thought I looked stunning in it and assumed everyone at the event thought I did, too. In retrospect, it was downright comical. At our 50th reunion, just being alive made one successful. It was fun. No pretensions there, just an honest realization that we are who we are. Age has a way of peeling away the piffle that clutters our youthful years. I now realize I spent many of my "peacock" years painting over my weaknesses and shining up what I perceived to be my strengths. That was okay, because it was important that we felt good about ourselves while we competed to succeed in our dog-eat-dog American system. We needed to be good at what we did, look good while we did it, and feel good about ourselves as we gave life our best shot. In many cases, we were trying to put lipstick on a pig. As an aside, I remember when Kay and I were quite the social animals. Our group of friends loved to party. Our partying often included going to clubs where we danced until the wee hours of the morning. I loved to dance, and, frankly, thought I had mastered fast dancing, so much so that I was amazed that other dancers didn't surrender the dance floor to me completely. In my mind, the other dancers should have stopped dancing so they could just watch me steal the show. In the case of dancing, I had let my ego lead me down the path of false assumptions and self-evaluations. We outgrew our clubbing/dancing years and, in essence, retired to our sofa. I hung up my dancing shoes thinking I had retired as the undisputed best dancer of my era. I lived in that bubble of ignorance until one night when an imminently danceable song came on our television and stirred me to action. I jumped off the sofa and told Kay to join me on the "dance floor" where we could step back in time and cut a rug. She didn't budge, and, instead, turned me down flat. Disappointed and deflated, I plopped back down on the sofa. After sulking for a few minutes, I asked Kay why she wouldn't dance with me. In her ever-present matter-of-fact style, she hit me with,

"Scott, we've been together since high school, and we have now been married for more than 50 years. For all those years, I have wanted to tell you that you are not now, nor have you ever been, a good fast dancer. In fact, you may be the worst fast dancer I have ever seen. I like slow dancing with you, but I will never again fast dance with you. I love you. Now let's be quiet and watch television."

Since that bubble-bursting incident with Kay, I have felt the urge to call every girl and woman I have ever fast-danced with to offer an apology. While Kay's revelatory frankness about my fast-dancing ineptitude was ego-crunching, I survived. I even grew to appreciate the fact that our advancing maturity enabled us to speak the truth—the plain old stripped-down, unvarnished truth. Old age, in a weird way, has set us free to realize the simple truth has a shine of its own.

I think many of us who were caught up in the work scene during our most productive years longed for confirmation of our value to the world. We wanted that pat on the back that implied we were doing okay. We wanted recognition for our work ethic, our intelligence, our wit, our skills, and our ability to compete favorably in the capitalistic workplace. Exaltation at any level was appreciated. Smart, loving family members and friends recognized our need for those words of encouragement and passed them on to us as fodder for our work energy.

It has been interesting to observe how differently men in my age group have handled retirement. Some have greeted retirement with open arms and a massive sigh of relief. They figuratively plopped down in their easy chair as if it were a great reward for their having survived the rat race. Just watching them slink into retirement makes me think that, in their case, the rat won. Some of them have became so mellow and cornball philosophical, they bore the world around them. They now seem hell-bent on becoming sweet old men who have parked their lives in neutral. I'll be happy to drop off my friends who have marshmallowed out on life at the senior center for their bingo game. Me? I'm still looking for action, though, admittedly, the action I seek is more cerebral than physical these days. I am big on old adages, and one that comes to mind that seems to fit my mood of the moment is, "I'd rather wear out than rust out."

On the other end of the spectrum, some of my elderly friends got so hooked on the competitive spirit, they can't quit competing. Competition is manna for their very existence. They seemingly thrive on adding to their abundant successes and love to test themselves over and over again. They are not idiots. They recognize they are no longer entering the arena with their A game, but they still think they can conquer their competition. These firebrands make lousy losers. Their enthusiasm for constant action is exhausting to those around them. If the competition thinks it has beaten them, it just doesn't realize the contest isn't over. I have a dear friend who is in his mid-eighties, and he still answers the bell when opportunity knocks. His name is Mort, and his knowledge of economic theory and existing economic conditions is phenomenal. When I started writing this book, I asked Mort if he could cite any humorous aspects of aging I might use. He looked at me like I was nuts and responded with conviction, "There's not a damn thing funny about getting old." Mort never leaves one wondering what he thinks.

Somewhere between the can't-wait-for-retirement people and the ones like Mort who will dine on entrepreneurial challenges until they die, us average folks can be found. We have wound down, but we've not fully surrendered to the inactivity that can accompany old age. With our wind down, most of us have weaned ourselves from the need for pats on the back and expressions of amazement at our prowess and accomplishments. We have downwardly adjusted our desires and expectations for praise since we now do very little to earn them. We simply aren't as productive as we once were, and our new-found inactivity is totally unremarkable.

This failure to engage in new and exciting activities causes many of us to fall into traps that eat away at our vitality and make us dull and conversationally crippled. With few or no new things to talk about, we drift into talking in the past tense. We swap action verbs for passive verbs. Before long, we've told all of our old stories, and with no new adventures to talk about, we start repeating our golden oldies. We talk a lot about dead people. My friends at the Fitness Center, Buck, Marshall, Paul, Carlo and I are so bad about repeating stories we've given each other permission to stop us if we start-off on a tale twice-told. I do think that if our past was good to us, we've earned the right to re-visit it whenever we choose to do so. Those good memories can help us reaffirm the good parts of the life we've lived and doing so helps us maintain a positive attitude. I, also, think it is only fair and just that I acknowledge the fact that poor health can sideline any dynamo. All any of us can do is to go, go, go, until we are stopped.

In writing this book on aging, I struggled to describe the challenges that come with surrendering our youth without suggesting we should just wave the white flag and quit living life to its fullest. Getting old has its humorous moments, but, for the most part, it's a deadly serious process. It changes everything about one's life. Eliminating one's birth and one's death, I would say puberty and aging are the two primary processes we go through that are powerful enough to re-direct one's life. The changes prompted by puberty, in essence, are fun and exciting (though often confusing and frustrating). They signal our passage into a new and fulfilling stage of life. On the other hand, aging facilitates changes that just aren't that much fun. The accompanying changes signal the end of many—not all—of life's fun and rewarding happenings, and they remind us of endings, not beginnings. This sense of finality that keeps bouncing around in an old person's head—in my opinion—is one of the key reasons our churches are full of old people. Mortality is too far in the future for many young people to feel a sense of urgency to cozy up to God. That's not the case with senior citizens. We know our time left on Earth is limited and getting active in our churches is akin to cramming for final exams. Since we don't have a lot to look forward to on this earth, we want to believe in Heaven, and we are trying to close out our lives in a style that pleases God and earns us passage through the pearly gates in case not everyone is admitted.

In general, I believe life keeps us so busy we don't have time to just sit around and contemplate every aspect of living. Now, when I try to sort through the complexities of old age, I find I tend to think in terms of lists. One list that keeps popping into my brain is one listing the false assumptions I had about getting old. That list is as follows:

- I assumed it would take longer to get old;
- I assumed I would always be cool and agile;
- I assumed I would never drive like an old person;
- I assumed I would always be able to have sex;
- I never assumed I would have to rely on mercy hugs for my contact with women;
- I assumed my sense of fashion and style would never be replaced by my desire for comfort;
- I assumed I would always be able to eat fried chicken, gravy, and ice cream; and,
- I assumed when I got old and wise, young people would cherish the pearls of wisdom I would pass on to them. Truth is, by the time I got pretty wise, my wisdom wasn't particularly relevant to today's world.

Being all philosophical in my writing makes me itch. Knowing I am not qualified to authoritatively advance philosophical notions, I am most uncomfortable doing so. With that discomfort in mind, allow me to move into areas I do feel qualified to talk about. First, here are some of the things I now value and enjoy greatly that I seldom took time to acknowledge before:

- a truly good book, especially British mysteries;
- television documentaries that involve, large animals, outlaws, World

War II, art, explorers, gems and rocks, Texas, major league baseball of
the 1950s, antiques and religious history;

• British mysteries on PBS television;
• mules;
• letting things go, or the ability to forgive;
• my "around-the-house" uniform;
• phone calls from old friends and family members;
• visits to old downtown areas in small towns;
• fainting goats;
• silence;
• New York Times crossword puzzles;
• birds (except for grackles);
• Jeopardy on television; and,
• seeing or talking to my children and grandchildren.

I need to explain four or five of those items I listed above, so let's start
with mules. My dad and my Uncle Curly, who were raised on farms, both
liked mules, and they passed that trait on to my two older brothers and me.
Daddy and Curly liked mules because they worked hard and were strong.
I like mules because they are unique in that they are hybrids and ended up
smarter and stronger than either of their parents. I like the fact that mules
have an independent streak that leads some to call them ornery. I think
mules wake-up thinking about who they are going to piss off that day and
how they are going to go about it. Daddy always told us boys that mules
were the very best at plowing a straight row. He did, however, warn us that
if a mule had any kind of vitamin shortage and there were fresh-cut stumps
in the field where you were plowing, the mule would quit plowing and head
straight for the stump. He would then begin to gnaw and suck on it. Daddy
added that there was nothing you could do to divert the mule from the
stump until it had its fill of whatever it was extracting from it. Daddy told
us stump-sucking mules weren't as valuable as the ones that plowed through
their diversions. If Daddy said it, it was true. If you visit zoos, you'll notice
monkey cages draw the most visitors. People like to look at monkeys. If you
go to a farm, you'll notice most people like to stare at the mules. For some
reason, monkeys and mules are just fun to look at. In the past, I did not take
the time to enjoy mules. I do now.

Now, about my "around-the-house" uniform. I know most people
have a "uniform" they jump into the minute they can sacrifice fashion for

comfort. I'm no different. My uniform is made up of a pair of old, worn-out cotton shorts, three cotton t-shirts that have been washed so many times they are softer than a baby's butt, and a pair of loose-fitting Nike flip flops. The fact that I have a uniform is hardly worth mentioning. The fact that I have three interchangeable t-shirts because I inevitably drop food on which ever one I'm wearing at mealtime is worth mentioning. My inability to get my food from my plate to my mouth mystifies me. It's an affliction I added to my repertoire when I hit 70. My hands don't shake, and I don't seem to have any physical justifications for being so messy. I suppose it should just be written off to my failure to pay attention to the task at hand, aided by the fact that I eat with my plate in my lap while sitting on my sofa watching television. In this matter and others, too, I've noticed my ability to keenly focus has now become a bit fuzzy around the edges. Just one more of those irritating little nuisances that come with the aging package.

If you read my list of things I value and enjoy now that I'm a senior, your eyebrows probably arched when you read "fainting goats." I understand your surprise, so let me explain. Kay and I spent a number of summers in Bend, Oregon. When there, we made a point to explore much of Oregon and we took many hikes through, around, and over lots of its trails. On several of those exploratory trips, I noticed herds of goats. I've always liked goats and just watching them has always been fun. It was fun, but nothing super special until…well, until I saw the occasional goat just fall down for no apparent reason. As I watched the herd, I noticed that more and more of the goats would just suddenly stiffen and then fall over, where they stayed for no more than a minute or two. The falling goats would then hop back up and go on about their business, while other members of the herd seemed to take turns repeating the drama over and over. I was mesmerized and I pulled off the road and parked on numerous occasions so we could watch this hysterical drama replay itself repeatedly. It seems that a number of the Central Oregon farms had herds of these peculiar goats. They are called fainting goats. I had never heard of fainting goats, but I am totally glad Noah put a pair of them on his ark. They tickle the dickens out of me, and I could watch them for hours. I read their faints are caused by mini-panic attacks. After watching various herds for hours on end, I can tell you it must not take much to panic a fainting goat because they go down often and easily. Sometimes I would honk my horn just to panic the herd. I love those little rascals. If I owned a few acres, I'd have a small herd of fainting goats, and I would invite my friends over to join me in watching them stiffen, faint, and recover. It's good for the soul. I should also admit that it doesn't take a whole lot to entertain me anymore. By the way, I am very glad humans don't faint when they panic.

I put "silence" on the list because it has only been recently that I've discovered the beauty of silence. I now understand why the old adage "silence is golden" has hung around so long. This proverb is believed to have first been written in ancient Egypt; but it was the Scottish poet, Thomas Carlyle, who first translated it for us. In 1831, he wrote, "Silence is golden, speech is silver." The clear meaning of the proverb is that saying nothing is preferable to speaking. A moment of silence is very informative in that it enables us to better know and understand ourselves. I now know I have spent far too much of my life with my mouth open. Hard for us to learn when we're talking. To my way of thinking, our society is desperately in need of silence. It is common knowledge that we suffer from an unrelenting bombardment of information, much of which we do not want to receive and is useless. I've put together an incomplete list of the sources of information with which we now have to contend. Look it over and add to it if you like. Here it is:

- television and radio—shows, advertisements, news, political commentaries,
- computers;
- email;
- Facebook;
- Google;
- LinkedIn;
- YouTube;
- Flickr (pronounced "flicker);
- Pinterest;
- Twitter;
- Snapchat;
- Instagram;
- TikTok;
- Tumblr;
- Reddit;
- WhatsApp;
- billboards;
- political signs;
- many sermons and speeches;

- telephone—a vast majority of the calls are unwanted, maddening, and automated;
- smart phones—texts, advertisements, etc.;
- conversations;
- machines—automated teller machines, restaurant ordering machines, etc.;
- newspapers—the majority of which seem to be politically oriented;
- the U.S. mail—most of which is now advertising material;
- newsletters;
- bumper stickers;
- signage—on buses, benches, cars, utility poles, store windows, etc.;
- books (like this one) and magazines;
- computer discs; and,
- other sources I can't think of right now.

You get my point. We suffer from information overload. This onslaught of information is a dramatic change from the simpler times in which I grew up, and it has left some casualties in its wake as it broke into our lives. All of this new information has undoubtedly made us smarter, and I do like the fact that the answer to about any question I can conjure up is instantly available somewhere in my computer. While I can celebrate the advantages of the emergence of the information age, I can also mourn the costs we've had to pay for it. I fear that among the carnage left by the tsunami of information we've seen is the carcass of an old friend. That friend is silence. Silence has served us well since the dawning of life. It has been the room we figuratively stepped into when we needed to clear our heads, needed to think, needed to resolve, needed to reconcile, and needed to pray. The time we spent in silence was a healing time and a time to re-charge our batteries. I believe we need to resurrect silence and give it ample time in our busy, noisy lives so it can nurture us and help us keep our sanity in a world that sometimes seems hellbent on implosion.

My friend, Dr. Richard Wing, once said in a sermon, "The power of a pause is awesome." My dad was less eloquent than Dr. Wing, when he used to say to me, "Shut up and listen." Both were right. Shh, I'm in a pause. Won't you join me? You will love the quiet solitude.

The last item on my list I'll offer insight on is "letting things go." This saying is rather self-explanatory, but I will mention a few things that improve our lives when we let go of them. I've always had a volatile personality that made it easy for me to hang on to anger, grudges, and stupid notions.

I wasted a lot of time letting angry thoughts and unfair judgements hold my mind—and therefore, my happiness—hostage. As I said earlier, learning the power to forgive is immensely freeing. I may have been a slow learner, but I did discover that if we fill our brains and hearts with love and good thoughts, we won't have room left over for bad thoughts and hatred. Bad thoughts and hatred just plain screw up a person's happiness. I have also noticed that a person's mood is highly contagious. I would much prefer to give another person an aggressive case of happiness than a case of unhappiness. Wouldn't you?

My favorite comic strip is PICKLES. It is a syndicated comic strip by Brian Crane that features Opal and Earl, an elderly couple just coping with the everyday oddities, challenges, and events that come with being old. Last week, I read a PICKLES that fit right into this chapter of "Adjusted Desires and Expectations." In it, Earl is telling his friend that he has had a good day because he didn't brush his teeth with Ben Gay, the shower head didn't fall off while he was showering, and he didn't lock himself out of his house when he went out to get the morning paper. I hear you Earl. Like Earl, we have adjusted our desires and expectations.

Many of a young man's desires and expectations are well known. Success, money, good health, and sex are a few desires and expectations that spring to mind. As we age, we don't willingly discard those desires and expectations. They just seem to be taken away from our realities somewhere along our paths to old age. We make lots of adjustments in our lives as we age, and, more often than not, our adjustments mean turning the dial backward instead of forward.

I never once expected a good night's sleep and a good bowel movement to have so much influence on the quality of my day. As I've noted elsewhere in this book, getting old is full of surprises.

SEX AND OTHER UNMENTIONABLES

This chapter on sex and other unmentionables is one of the shortest chapters in this book. That very fact tells the story of seniors' sex better than anything I could write, but I will still give it a shot.

When I think of how much I wanted to have sex after puberty hijacked my brain, I laugh at my youthful futility and wasted energy. When I think of all of my middle years of enjoying sex, I smile in contentment. When I think of the rarity, oddity, and prolonged absence of sex in my old age, I weep. I don't really weep. I just fall back on my memories of sex in my middle years and re-smile. The vast differences between those three stages of my sexual journey prove to me that God has a sense of humor. His game of waving the carrot in front of us, letting us chew on the carrot for a while, and then taking the carrot away from us is both bizarre and humorous. Could it be that His sense of humor has a mean side to it?

It's somewhat amazing to me what a huge thing sex has been in most men's lives. I can't speak for women, but, with a few exceptions, I feel safe in suggesting that women didn't sign over their lives to thinking about sex and pursuing it with full gusto like many, many men did and do. By the time we men are in our mid-seventies, we have burnt a lot of brain cells thinking about sex. If we were lucky, we also spent a lot of energy in performing the physical act of sex over the years. In a man's biological prime, sex was like thunder and lightning. In his old aga, it's like a slow drizzle in a dense fog. One could safely assume the Lord gave us sex so we would have a means of populating the earth. While we've done a pretty good job of that, I think the original purpose of sex has now taken a backseat to the sheer pleasure of having sex. Of course, our history studies tell us the ancient Greeks and Romans probably had more fun with sex than the law allowed. Back then, their sex obsessions were what we now call debased. Today, they would be turned into a television series.

Getting old definitely slows down a man's sex drive. It eventually impairs a fellow's ability to perform, too. Oh, some men maintain their sexual activity longer than others, but, eventually, every man's capacity to perform will "soften" to the point of putting him on the sidelines. Little blue pills and pumps have stepped up to extend the joys of sex for many men, but others just accept Nature's verdict and let sex fade into the memory zone. An old friend of mine told me recently that his wild oats have turned into prunes and All Bran. I hear you, brother.

I spoke with several nursing home administrators in Texas about whether or not there was sexual activity among their residents. In the words of Gomer Pyle, "Surprise! Surprise! Surprise!" The answer was yes. It seems the sexual urge and ability to perform of some of our homebound elderly is alive and well, and the sharing of intimacies still "pops up" on their to do lists. As I said, the administrators I spoke with were all in Texas. I don't know if the level of activity is the same in the other states as it is in the Lone Star State or not. It's possible Texans hang on to their pleasures longer than others, or it's possible they aren't above exaggerating a bit.

I've noticed that the brain and the inability to sexually perform are not always in sync within the old man community. The brain, regardless of the age of the man, still gets stimulated by the sight of a sexy woman. Men seemingly never lose the connection between sexy women and the resultant thoughts of sex. Apparently, men's ability to perform has nothing to do with their desire for sex. Quite often our brain screams "go" and our body screams "no." Men seem to hang on to the notion of trying to stay sexy more than women do as they age, perhaps because they perceive the loss of sex appeal dooms them to neutered status. I heard a comedian say, "women will never be equal to men until they can walk down the street…with a bald head and a beer gut, and still think they are sexy." That thrill-charged message of sex that once so excited our brains still happens, but, today, when it heads south, it usually runs out of testosterone before it makes it below our waists. As someone once said, "the only groaning noises he makes in bed these days are because of his bad back or sore knees."

To illustrate the prominent role sex plays in our lives allow me to remind you of all the different ways sex—or the thought of sex—intersects with our daily lives.

- The movies. How many movies have you seen in the last 50 years (excluding Disney) that don't have a steamy sex scene or sexual sub-plot?
- Magazine advertisements. Most magazine ads are for women's products and whether they are for hair products, perfumes, clothes, or automobiles, they subconsciously—or overtly—suggest that if a woman buys this product, she will be beautiful, alluring, and successful.
- Television shows. How many female stars are unattractive or even

average? For the most part, they are usually gorgeous, desirable, and
alluring,
- Women's fashion. Surely everyone—not just men—has noticed that
young women are just a handful of thread from going around naked.
- News women and commentators are all beautiful (except on PBS) and
they flash their well-shaped legs while sitting on their sets. I think the
head of hiring at Fox News may be the new version of Hugh Hefner.
Wow! He sure knows how to pick 'em pretty.

We've all heard it said that sex sells. It must be because corporate
America constantly uses it to excess. I'm not really complaining, because
the spark still flickers in me. It may never start a fire any more, but it does
still flicker. Those suggestive ads? They make me think of sex, not about
buying the product they are trying to sell.

You know, it's really okay that the ability to perform sexually eventually
rides off into the sunset, because looking sexy enough to attract a partner is
a very tall order for an old man or old woman. What can an old man do to
look sexy? Nothing, except maybe throw a thousand dollars or a set of keys
to a new sports car on the bed. In politics, I guess having power makes one
attractive to some . Money, power, and fame seem to carry a little sex appeal
with them. By the time we get to be grandparents, we generally look like
grandparents. My grandkids often tell Kay and me that we are "so cute." Oh,
come on. Cute is for pets, babies, and old codgers.

It's too bad, but ugly often accompanies old age in men. A sense of
self-preservation keeps me from saying the same about women. You know
what keeps growing on the body of men for as long as he lives?

- the nose
- the ears, especially the lobes
- toenails and finger nails
- unwanted hair

How many of us have spent time wishing we had bigger noses or ears,
or wishing our nails would just keep on growing, or wishing for more kinky
hair in our ears or nostrils? I sure as hell haven't.

You know what does stop growing? Use your imagination.

I've always enjoyed the pre-sex activities like the cuddling, kissing,
touching, and hugging. Those intimacies are still available to us and always
serve to tighten the relationship. However, I will admit that some of the

hugging and intertwining of legs is now somewhat uncomfortable or down-right painful. Also, muscle cramps and bouts with gas can spoil a romantic encounter. Neither is very sexy, but both are inevitable. Old couples that are still very much in love are good at finding ways to replace sex with romance. There is a difference. I read that "the space between episodes of intimacy becomes longer (as we age), but the space between episodes of romance don't have to."

In August of 2020, Kay and I rented a charming, off-the-grid, cabin in the mountains of Montana. No phones, no television, no Wi-Fi, no neighbors, just a tiny log cabin right on the banks of a rushing mountain stream. In the morning, we sat at stream's edge and talked over our coffee as the stream babbled along. In the late afternoon and early evening, we enjoyed our chilled wine and conversation as the stream babbled on. Can you say romantic? One afternoon we sat on the porch reading and sipping wine while we rocked. Simultaneously we put our books down, held hands and talked about what fun we would have had at this cabin when we were younger. We rocked some and stared at the creek, and then went inside and got a little younger. There's a lot to be said for romance.

Aging brings changes. You bet it does, but some of those changes bring peace and new adventures. Sex has always been important and I guess it always will be. Fine with me, but, today, if you handed me a tube of KY Jelly, I'd probably spread it on bread and eat it.

A man's sex life doesn't disappear as long as he has an active succubus. Know what a succubus is? It is defined as a demon in female form or super-natural entity that appears in a man's dream to seduce him, usually through sexual activity. I would like to tell you more about my encounters with my succubus, but I've not had a visit from her since I was a teenager. At this point, I have to assume my succubus lost my address or prefers younger men. Pity.

PERSONALITY TRAITS OF THE ELDERLY

Regardless of our age, we all have different personalities, habits, beliefs, and preferences. Consensus seems to say that as we age, we drag those traits along with us. They just become older versions of our youthful traits and seem to shift into a slower gear. I read a study that spent money to find out that people fifty or older are more sedentary than those who are younger. Well, duh. Who would've "thunk" it?

I read an article in which Michael Watson, Director of Livable Communities at *AARP*, interviewed a large number of extremely old people to try to discover their keys to living so long. He produced an article detailing his findings. (11) He identified seven traits his sample had in common. Those traits were;

- productive, active lifestyle (including exercise);
- positive mindset;
- resilience and adaptability;
- healthy weight and overall nutritious diet;
- ability to balance stress;
- good self-esteem and stubbornness; and,
- close bonds and social relationships.

I know quite a few really old people and the ones who seem to be handling old age best do seem to share these characteristics. On the other hand, I know some whose make-up does not include a few of those traits. I know one fellow who seems only to have developed the one about being stubborn. He can be a real ass, but a lovable ass. He would be well-advised to lighten up his hard-heartedness or he could end up very old but mighty lonely. A self-assessment of where I stack up with this list of traits tells me I am in pretty good shape. However, my wife and kids may draw a different conclusion about how I grade out. They have told me from time to time that I'm a grouchy old man. When they do that, I generally bite their heads off.

Aging does influence and somewhat re-shape a few of our personality traits as we march through the years. No one seems to dispute the assertion that when one is in his seventies and eighties his personality shows increases in his sensitivity (feelings easily hurt), his suspiciousness, and his radicalism. Once again, I seem to be a prime example of that assertion. I always thought I would mellow out when I got older. I haven't. In fact, I've tended to become a bit more irritable and combative. Down deep, I suspect I've become a grumpy old man because I was a grouchy young man. It should also be pointed out that we are never too old to learn something stupid. I read in one of the many lists I browsed before writing this book, that even duct tape can't fix stupid, it just muffles the sound.

The highly respected *Journal of Gerontology* noted that when we reach our seventies and older, we experience "substantive physical and cognitive impairments and reduced intellect." I wish I had not read that, but in truth, I think they were right. I once was very good at the television show Jeopardy. I loved it because it gave me a chance to show off my intellectual prowess to my family and, most importantly, to my wife. I've never stopped trying to impress her and prove to her that she married the right guy. My fall from the top rung of the Jeopardy ladder started with my being slower with my responses than the contestants on the show. I simply couldn't think fast enough or organize my responses quickly. The next phase of my fall was that I couldn't think of the answers even though I knew them. Now, I often utter swear words to express my anger at my mental lock jaw. I should also admit that my fall from Jeopardy prowess culminated when I got to where I just didn't know many of the answers. I've never even heard of the pop singers, entertainers, and current movies they ask about. Bottom line? I'm just not as smart as I once was. Obviously, there is much more to learn today than there was fifty years ago. I cannot keep up with the information overload we now have. I will have to figure out some other way to show off for my bride, and the list of options available to me is getting smaller and smaller.

An organization called *Quora* that has the mission of sharing and growing the world's knowledge base recently published an article entitled, "Some of the Best Qualities of Elderly People." It primarily consisted of asking a question or making a statement about old age, followed by one elderly scholar's answer or response. The answer/response person was sixty-seven-year-old Cyndi Fink, a noted writer on aging from Santa Rosa, California. (12)

Here are some of the more interesting and revealing exchanges:

Q: Does wisdom come with old age?
A: No. Stupid young people grow up to be stupid old people.

Q: Does old age mellow you?

A: No. An unpleasant young person will become an unpleasant old person.

Q: I'm like fine wine. I get better with age.

A: No. I'm not. That's just stupid.

Q: Sex gets better with age.

A: The only thing I'll say on this subject is get it while you can.

Cyndi Fink is a straight-shootin' lady.

Along these lines, I am reminded of an old Henny Youngman joke. He said, "My grandma is over eighty and still doesn't need glasses. She drinks straight from the bottle."

Many of our little personality quirks irritate the hell out of our children and grandchildren. It bothers my son—who doubles as my business partner—terribly that I almost insist on eating my meals at or around the same time each day. If we are in a business meeting at my lunch time, I start getting antsy and try to speed up the meeting. He is terribly unregimented and I have become far more regimented in my senior years than I was when I was his age. I don't know why I am that way, but when it's lunch time, I say let's eat.

Have you ever noticed that most old people—me included—still have land lines for their phone service? Oh, we, also have cell phones, but having a land line just seems more substantial. I cannot yet completely trust wireless communications. Most of us still care more about checking our mail than we do about checking our email. That's kind of silly because our mail is almost exclusively advertisements and bills. It calls for a celebration when we actually get a letter in the mail, particularly if its handwritten. What a joy! If we do get a real letter, it's usually from another old person. "Thank you" emails just don't have the same impact that "thank you" notes do—at least to me. Speaking of letters, notice some time that most of us seniors still write in cursive. You will find that many seniors still prefer to read from a book than deal with an electronic reader. The only reason I now use a Kindle is because I can enlarge the print size for squintless reading. I blow up the print to billboard size. I do admit to missing the feel and smell of a printed book. Also, have you noticed that many of us still use wall calendars. It just seems risky to rely on electronic calendars to tell us when our next doctor's appointment is. Lastly, most senior men still prefer a map to a GPS. We would rather wrestle with folding up a map than learn how to use GPS. Suffice it to say, old habits die hard.

There was a time when I would lay awake at night and worry about what others thought of me. I seldom do that now. It's a little late for me to hit the panic button about the shadow I used to cast. Remember how we were taught to respect our elders? Well, I still do, but it's getting harder and harder for me to find one.

Here are a few more items from a list my friends Jan and Charlie sent me that may ring a bell for you:

- Talk to yourself. There are times you need expert advice.
- "In style" are the clothes that still fit.
- You don't need anger management. You need people to stop pissing you off.
- Your people skills are just fine. It's your tolerance for idiots that needs work.
- "On time" is when you get there.
- "One for the road" means peeing before you leave the house.

I would write more, but it's time for "one for the road."

WHAT OTHERS THINK OF US OLDSTERS

I recently saw a refrigerator magnet that featured the image of an old woman who said, "I still have a full deck. I just shuffle slower now." I chuckled but drifted off into wondering if that magnet reflected what most younger people think of us older people.

In researching the subject, I found the results of a study done by senior care referral service, *A Place for Mom,* that queried two thousand people between the ages of sixteen and thirty-four about what they thought about old people. Here are their top five stereotypes: (13)

- they can't drive;
- they are lonely;
- they can't get around very well;
- they are technology-challenged; and,
- they don't want to go anywhere.

There's some truth to those feelings, but those traits or tendencies should be taken with a grain of salt. Research shows that we do drive slower but safer in our golden years. Some of us with active social and family lives are not lonely. In fact, sometimes we are so busy we just wish we had more alone time. As to not getting around as well as we used to, that's generally a fact. We tend to err on the sides of careful and slow as we fear falling. We know that if we fall, our bones break easily. Are we technology-challenged? Some more than others, but I read that sixty-five percent of old people use Facebook daily. When I told one of my granddaughters this statistic, she laughed and told me, "Granddad, only old people use Facebook anymore." She added that most younger people now focus more on Instagram and Snapchat and a few other programs of which I've never even heard. Well, it matters little. I am in the thirty-five percent that doesn't even use Facebook, and to resurrect a very old joke, "I'm roadkill on the information highway." I am not technology-challenged. I am technology-overwhelmed.

We may not want to go everywhere, but we like to travel. We are just more picky about where we go now and who we go with than we used to be, and sometimes we are dependent on others to take us wherever we go.

Also, we occasionally sense that those inviting us to go somewhere would really be happier if we didn't accept their invitation. We fear slowing others down or being a "load" for them to cope with. Travel is a tad bit difficult for some of us. It can be quite an ordeal. Just packing and lugging my C-PAP machine, box of meds, hearing aid charger, etc., is a pain in the "arse." In my case, if we drive to the other side of town, I get jet lag.

I think old people are easy to make fun of and easy to laugh at. It seems to me that most movies portray old people as grumpy, lonely, deranged, or doddering. Walter Matthau comes to mind. Old folks are often the comic foils on television sit-coms. These characteristics feed the stereotypes that younger people have about us (refer to study cited above). I am fine with younger people questioning my abilities. It allows me to astound them when I get something right, and I like the kudos and looks of surprise that follow. Also, as a matter of fact, we really are guilty of doing some funny things and are a little mistake prone. If our shortcomings can bring laughter to a serious world, so be it.

The *AARP Bulletin* recently ran a story entitled, "AGEISM ALIVE AND WELL IN ADVERTISING." It cited a number of popular advertisements that "dissed" the older folks and portrayed them as buffoonish, forgetful stumblebums. (14)

Paul Irving, chairman of the *Milken Institute Center for the Future of Aging,* was quoted in the article as saying, "advertising that stereotypes older adults and reinforces negative biases is not harmless." (14) It helps shape the negative impressions many young people have of their elders and even tends to weaken the already fragile self-confidence of many elders who are wrestling with diminished skills and vulnerabilities such as memory loss, hearing, and vision impairments. No one likes to be laughed at, regardless of their age.

Advertisers are very, very careful not to—in any way—portray women, people of color, or members of the LGBTQ+ community in any manner that could be construed as critical or ridiculing. However, the elderly appear to be fair game, with little or no political or economic retribution coming as a result of their being teased or ridiculed.

Advertisers may be shooting a real golden goose by teasing, making fun of, or taunting seniors. They must have overlooked the fact that people fifty-five years old or older now control more than 70 % of all personal wealth in the United States according to the Federal Reserve's *Survey of Consumer Finances.* (15) Further, the Bureau of Labor statistics "show that older adults buy 56% of all cars and trucks, 55% of personal care products,

65% of health care, 68% of home maintenance and repairs, and 76% of all prescription drugs." (16)

Ageism in advertising isn't surprising when we realize the lack of age diversity among those who are actually creating the ads. *The AARP Special Report* said, "the median age for a manager in America's advertising agencies is 37, and the average age of a creative person in the industry is only 28…" (14) It makes very little sense to me that advertising decisions are made by "kids" who simply do not have the experience base that enables them to adequately address the richest market. These young people are bright and creative, to be sure, but, perhaps, they should be dreaming up and producing ads appealing to markets with whom they have experience and may better understand.

Mike Hodin, CEO of the *Global Coalition on Aging*, says, "Many advertisements treat older adults as dependent and in need of real help, rather than as a target market representing substantial revenue growth." (17) Mike is right. It seems as though about the only ads aimed at seniors relate to burial insurance, reverse mortgages, supplements that make wrinkles disappear or fend off aging, retirement/assisted living homes, and drugs or medical procedures that address medical issues and illnesses unique to golden agers. Erectile disfunction and leaky bladders get some attention, too. I understand why advertisers zero in on these age-specific conditions and problems, but have they forgotten old folks still eat cereal, travel like crazy, and are as prone to impulse buying as they were when they were 30? Of course, now they can afford it.

Aging is seen as a state of decline. One psychologist called old age "a kind of existential purgatory." As best as I can interpret that academic gobbledygook, I think it means that old people are in a time and place of purification (purgatory) and, while there, they must create their own being for his or her specific situation and environment (existentialism). I guess we are to spend our last years rounding out the sum and total of our lives in an effort to purify it in preparation for our death. Heavy, huh? It may not be important for us to over-analyze our old age. It is important to just keep on doing life.

I often heard women complain that when men get old, they are called distinguished, but when women get old they are simply called old women. I'm not really buying that notion. I have heard older women referred to as elegant, sophisticated, and other complimentary terms. I, on the other hand, have heard countless men referred to as rednecks, bubbas, and old farts. I have never heard a woman referred to as an old fart. Some older women who refuse to settle for men their own age or older are called cougars. Older men who pursue females who are considerably younger than they are get called old fools, leches, or worse. Now, the label "cougar" may not be particularly complimentary, but at least it does conjure up an image of one who is sleek, beautiful, graceful, and wily. The labels hung on men pursuing younger women are pretty rotten any way you look at them.

During my many googles for information on aging, I found lots of descriptions of old people in various articles and studies. In fact, there are so many descriptions, I am inclined to think there is no consensus on a definition or description of old people. I read one that said young adults think us golden agers are "little more than slow-walking, bad driving, hard of hearing, Matlock-watching, citizens." I feel as though they are way off base. Matlock is a darn fine show. Some make fun of old people's going to bed early and accuse us of being absent-minded. I usually tell them my bedtime isn't so early. It's three hours after I fall asleep on the sofa. I have noticed it now takes longer to rest than it did to get tired. Also, it's kind of funny, I don't remember being absent-minded. Young people seem to get pickier and pickier the older I get.

An article in *Psychology Today*, by Dr. Lawrence Samuel, asserted that old people are "generally deemed weaker, less attractive versions of their younger selves." Shocker!. Being as old as I am, I am too often inclined to dispute what others say about those of us who are long in the tooth. In truth, I am wrong when I react with hostility because most of those descriptions are spot on. The trick to making the most of our senior years is to acknowledge that these are our senior years but to not sit around waiting for them to end.

There have been lots of movies and songs that immortalized the beautiful journey into and within old age. They were usually love stories in which someone overcame life's obstacles and ended happily. They told of true love winning out and making all of the hardships crumble before the eternal power of love. Christians believe the love of Jesus Christ conquers all and paves the way for our eternal peace and happiness. We all love happy endings.

Movies like *Cocoon* (1985), *Up* (2009), *On Golden Pond* (1981), and *Harry and Tonto* (1974) bring us tears of happiness as old folks use their last years to correct the wrongs of their youth and close out their lives in joyous, happy adventures. They remind us that a little happiness and doing some good deeds in our final years make-up for the many mistakes we made during our pre-golden years.

The greatest song ever written about aging is "Where've You Been?" written by Don Henry and Joe Venzer and recorded by Kathy Mattea in 1989. (18) It's the love story of Claire and Edwin. The couple had never spent a night apart in their sixty years of marriage. On those rare occasions he was late for dinner, she would meet him at the door with the words, "Where've you been? I've looked for you forever and a day. Where've you been? I'm just not myself when you're away." Then Claire suffers from extreme dementia and doesn't remember her children or any other information about her life. She's put in the hospital and soon Edwin becomes very ill and is put in the same hospital, but they are in separate rooms on separate floors. Finally, Edwin is moved into Claire's room as they both near death. He then reaches over and takes her hand. She gently squeezes it and slowly turns her head toward him and softly says, "Where've you been? I've searched for you forever and a day. Where've you been? I'm just not myself when you're away." I love this story and have cried each time I've heard the song. As I write these words, tears are making it difficult for me to see clearly. That could easily be Kay's and my story.

To lighten the mood a bit, I should tell you not all songs about aging are sweet and beautiful. There's one that the singer fesses up to becoming ugly as he became old. Its title is "I Don't Look Good Naked Anymore," written by two members of the recording band the Snake Oil Willie Band. Now, if you are old, tell me you can't identify with that title. It's classified as a country rock song, but it should be filed under Realism. In it, Willie—who is old and fat and unkempt—says of himself that he is a "deep-fried double wide version of the man he used to be." He admits that his belly is so big he wears a shirt when he goes swimming and only makes love with the lights off. It's a great little ditty and can be heard and seen on YouTube. I wish I could have entitled this book "I Don't Look Good Naked Anymore."

All of us stew a little over the skills we have lost as we have aged. Even if we weren't very good looking when we were younger, we miss the days when we didn't have wrinkles, sagging skin, glasses, and hearing aids. When I'm honest with myself, I know I wasn't as smart as I tell my children I was. I know I probably wasn't as good of an athlete as I tell folks I was. And I know I wasn't as suave, charming, and good looking as I hint I was. I'm pretty sure I amplify my mediocrity. It's kind of fun; plus, I don't really think people believe my exaggerations.

The older we old people get, the more we worry about being a bother to our children or caretakers. It's not a waste of worry, because we really are often guilty of putting a hitch in their get along. We know they are busy and that it puts a strain on them to deal with us. Our frailties, idiosyncrasies, stubbornness, forgetfulness, and inabilities are tough for our kids to see in their once strong and decisive parents. They would be well advised to realize we are very much aware of our shortcomings and are often embarrassed by our fall from family leadership. The kids need to be patient when dealing with our fragile self-images, and we need to be patient with their impatience.

Several folks posted an essay called "When Parents Get Old…" on Facebook that needs to be reprinted here. I don't know who originally wrote this item that was shared on Facebook, but it bears reading and thinking about. Here it is:

"When Parents Get Old…"

"Let them grow old with the same love that they let you grow…let them speak and tell repeated stories with the same patience and interest that they heard yours as a child…let them overcome, like so many times when they let you win…let them enjoy their friends just as they let you…let them enjoy their talks with their grandchildren, because they see you in them…let them enjoy living among the objects that have accompanied them for a long time, because they suffer when they feel that you tear pieces of this life away… let them be wrong like they didn't embarrass you by correcting you…LET THEM LIVE and try to make them happy the last stretch of the path they have to go; give them your hand, just like they gave you their hand when you started on your path!"

This little essay may not be well punctuated or it may not be written in a way that thrills a grammarian, but it's real life. It preaches a doctrine of patience, understanding and love, and those are very good doctrines to be floating around in our universe.

Final analysis, I am who I am, and I am what I am.

STUFF, AND WHAT TO DO WITH IT

As we march, or limp, into old age, we drag a lot of stuff along with us. Once we realize we are ensconced in old age and there is no turning back, we look around and realize how much stuff we have accumulated. Then, somewhere along the way, we wonder what the hell are we going to do with it all?

Two definitions of "stuff" are worth mentioning here. First, "stuff" is defined as "things used for some purpose." The second definition of "stuff" declares that "stuff is the essence of some abstract thing." Both of those definitions leave one scratching their head but, in a weird way, they both kind of fit the stuff we accumulate on our trip through life. Our stuff is special. The "purpose" it serves is to re-connect us with our past memories and the good times we had. The "essence of some abstract thing" means our stuff helps us measure the quality of life and love we have experienced as we passed through the different phases of our life. The "abstract thing" it refers to is happiness.

Mementos from our school days, crumbling and fading newspaper articles that had our names in them , our wedding pictures and kindred paraphernalia, too many photographs of our children, grandchildren, friends, old classmates, and family members—including cousins we barely remember—concert ticket stubs, notes and cards loved ones and special friends sent us long ago, vacation souvenirs, and odds and ends from our past are crammed into drawers and boxes. We don't re-visit these memory bins often, but it is very comforting to know they are near us and are available for visits when the mood strikes us. They serve as reminders that we have lived good and meaningful lives. In many cases, they are our rewards for the lives we have lived. I highly prize a drawer in my bathroom that is crammed full of birthday, anniversary, and thinking of you cards. They will be thrown away when I die, but not one minute before.

An element of old age can be bouts of melancholy. While experiencing those moments of low spirits, we often find solace in re-living the good parts of our lives. Visits to those memory boxes help us by taking us back to the "good old days." They soften our anxiety and give us gentle pats of reassurance, in a figurative way, when we need them.

Kay and I found ourselves wanting to simplify life as we crossed over into the golden years. That effort included downsizing in our home, buying fewer electronic services—especially those that require passwords, canceling many subscriptions, driving our cars longer, and trying to get rid of clutter and much of the stuff we have accumulated through the years. That latter chore has been much easier for Kay than it has been for me. She has attached herself to very few things in her life. She is just a people person, not a thing person. Me? I have attached myself to tons and tons of stuff, people, and things. I am not a hoarder by any stretch of the imagination, but I get awfully antsy when we go on one of those throw-stuff-away jags.

Most of us have had to go into the home of a deceased loved one to clean it out. In the case of elderly loved ones who have died, the chore is often heartbreaking and usually difficult. It feels as though we are intruding on that person's life and invading their privacy. Their secrets and private thoughts are revealed to us. Most of the clean-out work is mundane, but there are usually a few surprises.

I often think what it will be like for our two children to have to go through our stuff. I try to imagine what they will keep, and if they wonder why we kept this stuff all those years. I also think about which things might bring smiles to their faces, which things might bring tears to their eyes, and what they might quickly discard as unnecessary. Hoping to simplify their "clean out" task has inspired Kay and me to do as much filtering of stuff as we can. As I said before, Kay's better at clutter-clearing than I am. When we start one of those clean out sessions, I spend more time watching what Kay is trying to discard than I do adding to the trash pile. My reasoning goes something like this: I don't know when I am going to die so why throw stuff away I might want to re-visit soon? Now, if God whispers our expiration date into our ear before He takes us, I will make an energetic effort to get rid of stuff. That kind of thinking will inevitably lead to a big job for our kids someday. I just hope none of the secrets they learn about me disappoint them.

I've not only been a keeper of mementos, but I've also been a rather active collector of certain kinds of items through the years. If these collectibles fit the category of "stuff", they, at least, should be awarded a capital "S" in their spelling. I have enjoyed collecting the things I have and that makes it difficult to let go of them. I have long been a collector of the following things:

- sports hobby cards (since 1951);
- glass and agate marbles (since the early 1950s);
- hardbound books and first editions (since the late 1960s);
- small antiques (since the early 1970s);
- metal pins (the kind one pins on their clothes); and,
- original art.

My sports card collection was very large and took up lots of room. I knew neither of my kids wanted to house such a large collection and I assumed all of my four granddaughters would pass on the opportunity to be major sport card collectors. I sold the entire collection. My book collection was overflowing all of our bookshelves and my kids had their own collections, so I picked out eighty books I could live without and sold them to a book store that specialized in second-hand books. I made a whopping $100 but received some in-kind payment from Kay who applauded my effort at de-cluttering our house. Those sold books did not include any of my first editions. I have sold numerous antiques for pennies on the dollar, but, at least, my kids won't have to play *Sanford and Son*.

I still have all of my marbles (keep your opinions to yourself), metal pins, and art. The marbles and pins are small enough for someone to hang on to and the art will go into inventory at our family-owned art gallery.

Kay collected a few things but was never avid about it. She has a nice collection of tulip glasses that old timey Kraft Swanky Swigs (soft cheese) used to come in. For a while, she collected Depression Era green glass and Fiestaware dishes, most of which came from my mother's house after she passed away. She has since lost interest in those items, so I've been instructed to "move 'em out." However, I suspect one of our granddaughters will snap-up the Swanky Swig tulip glasses.

It is easy to tell an old person to "get rid of things." It is hard for an old person to do so. The sentimental tug a golden ager feels can be overcome, but most of the options for getting rid of "meaningful" stuff presents tough challenges. Because we have placed a value on what we have kept, our reasoning tells us to sell versus give away. Trying to sell stuff is a chore. Good stuff can often be consigned to second-hand shops or antique stores. However, making the sales calls is tough for some elderly folks, particularly when the merchant considering "taking" your stuff starts telling you how little you items are worth just to get your price down. Then, there are websites like eBay, Craigslist, Facebook, etc. Getting your goods on one of those electronic marketplaces seems like a major undertaking to old folks like me who tend to tense up when faced with an electronic task. My best option for getting my stuff on the web is to con one of my granddaughters into doing it for me.

Neat people don't have nearly as tough a job getting rid of stuff as us savers do. They simply don't have as much stuff to worry about. I don't know whether to envy those people or feel sorry for them. I sometimes wonder if they were so tightly wound that coloring outside the lines made them nervous. My stuff and things have been good friends to me as I've aged. I am happy I have never been one to confine my interests by living within strict guidelines. In admitting that, I know I have made many neat freaks' skin crawl. So be it.

Here are everyone's options for dealing with their stuff and things:

- donate everything that has value;
- throw all of your stuff and things away and focus on something else;
- sell what you can if you can avoid the nervous breakdown that often accompanies the effort; and,
- keep living as you are with all your stuff nearby and let your kids handle everything after you die.

Obviously, some combination of the above disposal options is probably the way to go. I am doing the full menu of options, but, truth be known, my kids will still have a helluva lot of work to do when I reach my end time.

GETTING OLD AIN'T ALL BAD

Most of the answers you would get if you asked an old person what was good about being old would generally be some iteration of one of the following three responses:

- nothing;
- the pressure to perform or excel is off—it's wind down and coast time; and,
- let me count the ways—each of us can enumerate several things such as "I am wiser now," "I now have time to do what I want, when I want," and, "I am happy."

When asked that question, my wife, Kay, rather quickly answered, "I can get out of bed when I want to." Different strokes for different folks. Some people respond to the afore-mentioned question with sugary, somewhat predictable responses, while they flash the look that whispers, "look how sweet I am now." I find responses like these to be so syrupy and staged that I want to blow them a raspberry. You might surmise from my response that one of reasons I enjoy old age is because I can sort of lift the lid of propriety. You'd be correct.

Old age comes with the freedom to be a bit of a scoundrel if one is inclined that way. We have spent our lives being shaped and molded by rules and ever-changing lists of do's and don'ts. Parents are the first ones to lay down rules for us to follow. Then schools and teachers hit us with a whole new set of rules the first day we set foot on campus. Coaches imposed their rules on us. Along the way, we learn that there are countless laws that have huge influences on what we can and can't do. Once we get out of school and join the work force, we are given new rules to follow that govern our conduct while working and representing the company we work for in the public eye.

When we marry, there are marriage vows and a host of unwritten rules that govern how we behave as a spouse. Linda, a strong-willed friend of mine who lives in Houston, told her husband Robert before their marriage to never tell her "no." She said that taking a firm stand like that would backfire and cause her to do exactly what she was told not to do. I guess he believed her because they've been happily married for many years. When children come along, we have many rules dealing with how we behave as responsible, loving parents. Plus, at this point, we start laying down the rules to our children and start the cycle all over again.

If one has been raised in the church, he or she has spent a lifetime trying to understand—and follow—the many rules governing our lives and telling us how to get along with each other and with God. As a kid, I felt like preachers tried to scare the hell out of me, not coax it out. As I grew older, I realized each preacher had his or her own interpretation of most of the religious rules. They were all people of God and meant well, but all of these different interpretations were often confusing and irritating.

I have spent more time than I would like to admit dancing on the edge of propriety. I knew the rules, but I willfully broke many of them for the sake of a good time. As a teen, I used to wish I was a Catholic, because rumor was they could do about anything and then get it expunged from their record by going to confession. I later learned that my Catholic friends didn't interpret confession the way I did. Their guilt was as heavy for them as mine was for me. As I aged, I learned that God will wipe my slate clean if I ask for forgiveness and mean it. He is a lot more lenient than some of the teachers and employers I had.

The point I am trying to make here is that in old age we have the freedom to quit worrying so much about some of the rules that attempted to govern our behavior. It, also, becomes much easier to follow the rules as old folks because it usually requires substantial energy to break the rules. Sinning is hard work and tiring, and I no longer have the energy to spare. When I look around our church on a Sunday morning, I mostly see sweet, calm, gentle elderly people. I grin to myself knowing that many of these people have broken rules in their younger lives, too. Some may still do so.

This new freedom we can enjoy in our golden years also enables us to tell more people "I love you'" than we once would have. I have a large core group of friends with whom I grew up. The fifteen-to-twenty of us talk to each other with some regularity even though we are spread all over the country. I started telling each of them "I love you" a few years ago, and now, all of them feel free to tell each other the same thing. I attribute this ease of expressing ourselves to our finally feeling secure in our own skin. We have forgiven each other for any misdeeds one may have inflicted on the other and we focus our relationship on today. We have discovered that it is not embarrassing to tell a friend, "I love you." Now that's a freedom we should all practice.

While on the subject of rules, I should point out that every set of rules I've lived under has been designed to help me and keep me out of trouble. I have always lived a rambunctious life. I needed the rules.

Sometimes we get a bit depressed by being old. That down feeling usually comes when we string together numerous aches, pains, and illnesses, or get frustrated by our inability to do something we used to do with ease. Times like those call for a self-remedy session I refer to as "count your blessings times." When I get to feeling sorry for myself, I usually go stare at our photograph wall. Each time I spend some time looking at the photos of the people I have loved and lost and those I still have around to love, my heart jumps on the joy highway and I enjoy the ride. I most always walk away from that wall thanking God and smiling. In my case, remembering the good parts of the life I have lived is manna that has sated my heart and medicine that has cured my blues.

I came across some articles that had lists of conditions caused by aging I found pertinent and interesting. The first one was entitled "Nine Things That Get Better with Age." It appeared in *The Heritage at Brentwood's Senior Living Newsletter.* (20) Here's their list:

- happiness;
- memory—some types actually do improve;
- decision making;
- stress—less of it;
- empathy;
- storytelling;
- self-confidence; and,
- wisdom, and
- positive mindset.

I can agree with most of their observations. Improving memory is worthy of a chapter unto itself. In my case, I've become quite proficient at telling my old stories. I can't remember who I've told them to so repetition is ingrained in the part of my memory that works. Do you suppose we become better at storytelling because when we get old, we tend to tell the same stories over and over? Well, practice does make perfect, or so they say.

The other list I found interesting was one entitled, "Eleven Things That Improve With Age." It was published by *LittleThings.com*. (21) Here we go:

- whisky;
- cheddar and Gouda Cheese—they do, however, get moldy;
- denim jeans;
- cast iron skillets;
- beef;
- balsamic vinegar;
- fine leather;
- pickles;
- flannel sheets;
- wine; and,
- seedlings.

This list amused me and it sent my mind in several different directions. First of all, I thought that perhaps I should drink more whisky while eating more steak cooked in an iron skillet with cheddar cheese melted on top with a pickle on the side. I should then take off my old jeans and fine leather belt and crawl into my flannel sheets for a good night's sleep. Would flooding my life with these things that improve with age cause me to improve in my old age via osmosis?

Regarding the seedlings, the article suggested that the seedlings would go on to create tall, strong trees and, ultimately, entire forests that would continue to expand long into the future. In so doing, they provide us with a metaphor for our lives in that we can grow to "plant" seeds that will result in young, strong offspring that will continue the process long into the future. The metaphor represents that we can become better versions of our younger selves as we reach the potential that is within us all.

By putting seedlings on the list, I am reminded that they must receive Nature's help in the forms of rain, sunshine, and protection from life-ending catastrophes to reach their potential and achieve their purpose in life. The metaphor that compares the seedlings to us further reminds me that for our young people to achieve their potential and realize their purpose in life, they must be nurtured during their formative years. A steady dose of love helps, too. It is our responsibility to provide this nourishment for our young, and for the good of mankind. Accepting that responsibility and acting on it yields tremendous rewards to us in our old age. It is thrilling to watch our young people grow strong and become good people. It also brings our lives full circle and gives them meaning.

Leon Trotsky said, "Old age is the most unexpected of all things that happen to man." I may not completely buy into Leon's quote, but I do know there have been an awful lot of surprises that accompanied my journey into old age. In general, I like surprises. I have always been one who saw the glass as half full. I even look forward to answering the phone when it rings. I do so because I "assume" it will be good news. Even though the preponderance of robo-calls have proven that ninety-nine out of one hundred calls are irritating and useless, I still answer the phone expecting good news. Oh, I have received the unexpected news of the death of a loved one. Doctors have occasionally delivered unexpected and unwanted medical news to me such as telling me I had to have by-pass surgery, my tests confirmed I had diabetes, I have sleep apnea and have to sleep in a Darth Vader-like mask, and my testosterone left me and caught the bus out of town, but all of that bad news received by phone hasn't yet robbed me of my optimism. I am not lost in la-la land. I know good news is a bit harder to come by as we age but, so far, these unexpected bad medical messages may have reminded me of my mortality, but make no mistake about it, I'm still high on life and I still believe that when the phone rings, it will be good news.

As I was reading through my wife's high school alumni website (Marshall, Texas, 1965) I ran across a list called "Perks of Being Over 70." I don't know what wit came up with it, but I think it's worth sharing. Here we go:

- Kidnappers are not interested in you;
- In a hostage situation, you are likely to be released first;
- People call you at 9PM and ask, "Did I wake you?"
- People no longer view you as a hypochondriac;
- There is nothing left to learn the hard way; and,
- You can live without sex, but not your glasses.

As I write this book on aging, I am repeatedly reminded that our attitude defines how we age and how we deal with the harsh changes that come with it. I don't know how to help people adjust their attitude. Heck, I'm not even sure I do such a great job of managing my own. I can only suggest that it is time well-spent to dedicate some of your time to standing before your own family photo wall. Also, trust God. Lastly, look upward with confidence.

THINGS THAT HELP MAKE DEATH TOLERABLE

Very, very few people want to die. Even the most downtrodden of us can usually find bits and parts of life that make it worth living and makes us happy. Christians call these good bits and parts of life blessings. Doubters or non-believers call them good luck.

I have had a few elderly friends tell me they wish they could die. They were either very ill, very lonely, or were just plum tuckered out. When my brother, Robert, was on his death bed and could only whisper, I leaned down and asked him if he was ready to "go." He responded so softly I could barely hear him. He said, "No, I'm gonna fight for every breath." In most of us there is a strong will to live right up until our last breath.

I also know quite a few folks that accept death's inevitability and profess to be ready for its coming. I don't know if I believe them or not. Sometimes I think they are just trying to prepare themselves for their passing. Faithful people of God have convinced themselves that Heaven awaits them and that will be eternal happiness. They have confidence that life as we know it has a happy ending. I tend to be in their camp. Being in that camp gives me a certain ability to face death with no fear. The former radio commentator, Larry King (who was Jewish, by the way) once posed the question, "If all of these people believe in Heaven, why aren't they eager to die?" Could it be that Larry had a valid point about our unspoken views of life after death? Do some of us believers maintain an iota of doubt about the afterlife?

Everyone has to face the coming of death in their own way.

This chapter has evolved into a somber collection of thoughts and paragraphs. Let me inject a little levity into it by sharing a list of things I think will help make dealing with death a bit more tolerable. Here's my "No More" list:

- no more rap music
- no more tattoos
- no more celebrity political comments
- no more worrying about your health
- no more gangs
- no more pedophilia
- no more doctors' appointments

- no more television advertisements
- no more New York Times
- no more prejudice
- no more war
- no more starving children
- no more greed
- no more medicines to take
- no more untimely and embarrassing gas
- no more mistakes
- no more kale
- no more corny poetry
- no more pain
- no more mosquitos, roaches, or houseflies
- no more addictive drugs or alcohol
- no more crime
- no more bumper stickers that say "I love my (dog breed)"
- no more weeds
- no more stairs
- no more terrorism
- no more pimples
- no more embarrassing moments
- no more robo calls
- no more political calls
- no more phony charity calls
- no more little dogs that yap too much
- no more national championships for the University of Alabama
- no more whining from Ohio State
- no more jumping cholla cacti
- no more social media
- no more traffic jams
- no more misuse of "I" and "me" or "myriad"
- no more feminization of the male gender
- no more muffler-less motorcycles
- no more having to hear "The Twelve Days of Christmas"
- no more dental appointments
- no more parsley
- no more opera
- no more snobbery
- no more haircuts
- no more tailgaters
- no more silly lists

My list of "no mores" may raise some folks' hackles, but it's totally subjective and listing them was therapeutic. Your list of "no mores" may be quite different from mine, but the point is, death brings us relief from some of the bad things and plain old crap that haunts us and taxes our happiness. Some folks would spell that "r-e-l-i-e-f."

As I noted somewhere else in this book, writing it has made me think of different lists. I am not certain the following list of Sayings I'm Tired Of Hearing belongs in this chapter—or even this book—but death will bring me relief from hearing these over used clunkers.

- take it to the next level
- lay it on the line
- in the hunt
- man cave
- they control their own destiny
- I'm a hugger
- the cutting edge
- give 110%
- the ball is in his/her court
- to the right of Attila the Hun
- it tastes like chicken
- we're a nation of immigrants (to be accurate, we should say we are a nation of *legal* immigrants)
- hi there (Where is there? Why not, "hi here?")

Since I just listed some words and phrases I am tired of hearing, it seems appropriate to list some phrases and sayings I wish would make comebacks. The only thing these items have to do with aging is that they are as old or older than I am. Remember these?

- useless as teats on a boar hog
- where's the beef?
- the buck stops here
- madder than a wet hen (or hornet)
- phony as a three-dollar bill
- the Golden Rule
- fast as greased lightning
- cold as a witch's teat in a brass bra
- can't make a silk purse out of a sow's ear
- holler like a stuck pig

- soft as a catfish's belly
- tighter than Dick's hatband
- busier than a frog on the freeway with a broken hopper (Tennessee Ernie Ford)
- as thrilling as kissing your cousin
- more fun than a barrel of monkeys
- crazy as a bedbug
- stronger than strained horse piss
- as loud as a cow pissing on a flat rock
- a roll in the hay
- dumber than a box of rocks
- meaner than a junkyard dog
- plum tuckered out (used earlier in this chapter)
- tighter than Aunt Tilly's purse strings
- drunker than Cooter Brown
- sleep tight and don't let the beg bugs bite
- Whatever you think, don't ever, unless you will (Ray Stevens)
- born under a lucky star

This list maybe adds little to the academic value of this book, but, what the heck? Consider it a dose of fun in a book that deals with a serious subject.

So much of this book deals with change and how it affects the aging process. The high-tech revolution, medical breakthroughs, political correctness, a soft-on-crime judiciary, social sensitivities carried to the extreme, class warfare, police reform, the proliferation of harmful drugs, etc., etc., have been exceptionally hard for many old people to come to terms with.

Many of us read these trends as slaps in our faces because they are different from the way we did things in our time. Oh, we will admit we did not get everything right, but we are stressed by what we perceive to be a rush to throw out of the good with the bad. There are countless things happening that lead us to conclude our time is past. It's okay. It's even rightfully so. It's just tough to be turned out to pasture.

All of these rapid-fire changes have brought countless changes to our language. Here are a few words and phrases I never heard until I hit sixty:

- emotional support animals
- tofu
- tiny houses
- reflexology (old word; new to me)
- xenophobia

- living will
- misogyny
- roughage
- social media
- Keto
- opioid
- Flomax
- Brexit
- stool softener
- almond milk
- Obamacare
- Bitcoin
- undocumented worker
- streaming

I could have filled several pages with new medical and medicine words and names. I could have done the same with high-tech words. I decided not to because I just don't like them.

Old age gives us codgers the right to bitch and moan and reminisce about the "good old days." We are not complete idiots. We know the good old days were not that good, but we learned to cope during those times, and we haven't quite got the knack of coping with this new generation's world.

DEATH BY ANOTHER NAME IS STILL DEATH

"Death" is a sorry, ugly word. It has a tough job. It's not a happy word unless it's describing the fate of weeds, bad ideas, or things nobody likes. Research revealed a handful of definitions for the word "death," but the most common one appears to be, "the irreversible cessation of all vital functions especially as indicated by the permanent stoppage of the heart, respiration, and brain." Now that's dead. It probably took a committee of scholars to come up with that definition. We all know what death means, so I wonder why we pin definitions on words of which everyone knows the meaning.

Some people are so repelled by the words "dead" or "death" they generally avoid saying them. For those folks, there are hundreds, if not thousands, of substitute words for saying someone is dead or muttering the word death. Wikipedia has a near endless list of words and phrases that mean died, dead, or death. The many listed below are truthfully a very incomplete list and they come from everywhere and nowhere specifically. The list is long, but kind of fun, if death in any form can be fun. Here's the list:

- the big sleep;
- done for;
- kicked the bucket;
- the big adios—actually comes from a Swedish saying that says, "Live life to the fullest before the big adios!"
- bit the dust;
- fell off his perch;
- pushing up daisies;
- on the wrong side of the grass;
- bit the big one;
- bought the farm;
- cashed in his chips;
- wearing a pine overcoat;
- is history;
- gone to shake hands with Elvis; and,
- taking a dirt nap.

If you want to "wake-up" your obituary, use one or two of the above listed doozies. No one will be offended and, come to think of it, who cares if they are?

There are, also, a number of sweet, spiritual, and comforting phrases designed to reassure the grieving their dead loved one is going to be ok. Here are a few of those:

- promoted to glory;
- at peace;
- at rest (a really long rest);
- beyond the veil;
- gave up the ghost;
- ascended to Heaven;
- joined his maker;
- earned her angel wings;
- gone to a better place;
- gone to one's reward; and,
- crossed the rainbow bridge.

It is irrelevant what we call death. If we want to control what is said about us in our obituary or memorial service we should script it. Lots of people do, partly to keep others from having to go to the trouble of doing it when they "go to shake hands with Elvis." They, also, may want to make certain they control the narrative and make sure some nice things are said about them. Most of us still cling to a little vanity when we get old, and we would like to be a fly on the wall at our own funeral. It would be fun—or angering—to see who shows up to pay their respects and see who doesn't. We would also like to hear what is said about us by our loved ones and friends. I suspect God keeps us in the dark about what goes on at our funeral to avoid hurt feelings.

Some people even get mummified so they can be seen by any ghoul seeking to see an old dead mummy. Vladimir Lenin died in the Soviet Union in 1924, and his embalmed body went on public display in Red Square shortly thereafter. It is still on public display. He may not technically be a mummy, but I think of him as a mummy without the wrapping. Others are put on display for long, long periods of time after they "bit the dust." I just don't know who they are or where they are, but there clearly seems to be a certain percentage of our population that is fascinated by death. What is it that makes so many of us interested in seeing old dead things? Hundreds of thousands of people walk by the dead Lenin for a peek annually. People pay big bucks for fossils, particularly fossilized dinosaur parts. Some collectors also spend good money to buy fossilized dinosaur poop. Someone—no doubt an expert on old turds—paid in excess of $10,000 for a fossilized dinosaur turd at an auction in July of 2014. I wonder if scratch and sniff works with old poop. Tell me there aren't some really weird people walking among us.

Are you familiar with cryogenics? It's a process that freezes dead people and adored pets and stores them in complex chemical solutions in a metal cylinder that is kept somewhere far south of freezing. The idea behind this "science" is that sometime in the future, medical science will advance to the point where it can thaw out the frozen body and cure the illness or disease that killed it. Next? Voila, the person or pet comes back to life and picks up where he left off. Some years ago, there was a big brouhaha between two factions of the family of the baseball great Ted Williams. When the Splendid Splinter, as he was known in the sports world, died, someone in his family placed his body in a cryogenic facility in Scottsdale, Arizona. Other family members wanted to thaw Ted out and bury him in the family plot. I don't know where Ted is now but he is not yet back in the Red Sox line-up.

There are all sorts of things going on with cloning—most of which is not known to the public. We all remember Dolly, the ewe that was cloned at the Roslin Institute in Scotland. She was the first mammal cloned from an adult cell. To my knowledge, no one has yet tried to clone a human, but the ability to do so cannot be far away. Start saving your money.

Cryogenics and cloning are early efforts to avoid the finality of death. Humans have always wanted to live longer, if not forever. The Spanish explorer, Juan Ponce de Leon, reportedly spent the best years of his life traipsing all over Florida looking for the mystical fountain of youth. I suspect he wasted those years and must not have found it because he died at the ripe old age of sixty-one. Death is a part of our lives (oxymoron?), and it is likely to remain that way far, far into the future. The philosophical cat Garfield, from the comic pages, once said, "As you grow older, you realize what's really important, like, for instance…not growing old." Well, Garfield, Ponce de Leon would agree with you.

Michael Meade, who billed himself as a mythologist and storyteller, said: "An old Celtic proverb said, 'Death is the middle of a long life.'" I wish the Celts—or Mr. Meade—had explained what they/he meant by their proverb. They didn't. However, since I have not seen any 150-year-old Celts walking around, I think they must have been talking about some kind of afterlife. I like believing in the afterlife. It fits comfortably into the future I designed for myself years ago.

WANT TO LIVE LONGER? WELL BE SHORT, OVERWEIGHT, HAVE A POSITIVE ATTITUDE, AND GO TO CHURCH

When I decided to write a book on aging, I planned on it being a mostly farcical look at the process. However, as I got into it, I kept bumping into aspects of aging that detoured me from my lighthearted intentions. Before long, I found myself researching issues of aging and the fate that awaits all of us agers—death. While there is still a lot of humor to be found and experienced in our getting old, there are some pretty weighty situations we need to be prepared to face.

At the risk of oversimplifying my findings, I have found some major aspects affiliated with aging that evolved into a bit of a table of contents for this book. Here are some of those topics:

- the inevitability of getting old;
- efforts to slow the aging process;
- factors that speed or slow the aging process;
- the effects of aging on our minds and bodies and the changes the process inflicts upon us;
- recognizing that the older we get, the closer we come to death;
- dealing with the approach of death; and,
- do we have a future after we die.

Just about everything I have studied and written about getting old and dying fits within one or more of the above-listed topics. To finish this manuscript, I need to quit finding angles of the aging and dying processes that interest me. That has proven far more difficult than I ever imagined.

Most recently, I tried to find out what effects, if any, height, weight, attitude, and religion have on our life span. My interest in this arm of research stems from the fact that I am 6'4" tall, am a little overweight, have a positive attitude, and attend church regularly. Since most of you have one or more of those characteristics, you might enjoy the following research results.

According to healthline.com, (8) "Researchers found that at age 70 years old, the taller men were expected to live approximately two years less than those who were shorter."

Men'shealth.com (22) says, "A 1992 study of nearly 1700 dead guys found that, on average, men shorter than 5'9" hung around 'til the ripe old age of 71. Men taller than 6'4", on the other hand, checked out around the age of sixty-four."

The Albert Einstein College of Health published a study in 2021 (23) showing that each additional four inches of height increases the risk of all types of cancer by 13% among post-menopausal women.

In social anthropologist Brian Palmer's article on the website, slate. com, (24) he wrote, "I don't blame short people for wishing on a star for height, or parents seeking out growth hormones for their size-challenged children. The sociological data is compelling at a surface level, and there are some concrete advantages to height...but the evidence linking height to life-threatening disorders should give us all pause." Well, I am now on pause. What's next? Palmer continued, "Tall people rarely live exceptionally long lives. On average. Japanese people who reach one hundred (100) are four inches shorter, on average, than those who are seventy-five."

I've been tall, relatively speaking, all of my life. You will find me in the back row of every class picture in which I appeared. I have thoroughly enjoyed my height, in spite of always having to change burned out light bulbs and having to help short people retrieve items from the top shelves at grocery stores. It helped me in sports, with girls, and in business. All of the time I was enjoying being tall, I never realized that my asset would prove responsible for shaving a few years off of my life expectancy. Now, I am officially on a thoughtful pause. Coming off of pause, I have concluded that, all things considered, I am glad I am tall. If you have a burned-out light bulb, I'm your man.

Most of us know that being severely underweight is unhealthy and can shorten life. What very few know is – that in some cases – carrying a few - and I do mean a few – extra pounds can actually help some older folks maintain their resistance to some maladies.

A religious leader in America, Norman Vincent Peale, wrote a book entitled *The Power of Positive Thinking* in 1952 that woke up the world about the value of going through life with a positive attitude. Since its publication, the book has sold more than five million copies and continues to sell at a brisk pace. Some scholars have hailed *The Power of Positive Thinking* as one of the most influential books ever written.

Does a positive attitude affect life expectancy? My research into that question led me to countless studies, articles, and opinions, all of which answered the question with a resounding "yes." Per the Mayo Clinic in an article written by Mayo staff that appeared in mayoclinic.org, (25) "health benefits that positive thinking may provide include:

- increased life span;
- lower rates of depression;
- lower rates of distress;
- greater resistance to the common cold;
- better psychological and physical well-being;
- better cardiovascular health and reduced risk of death from cardiovascular disease; and,
- better coping skills during hardships and times of stress.

I do not know whether people are born with positive or negative charges. I've known lots of very bright people who always saw the proverbial glass as half empty. I've, also, known lots of optimists. All things considered, I would much rather hang out with the optimists than the dark cloud guys. It seems to me that most negative people aren't really happy until they rain on someone's parade or tread on someone's dreams or hopes. Positive people, on the other side of the coin, encourage others and spread hope and cheer.

Does believing in God and having a good relationship with Him add to our years on earth? Ohio State University conducted two surveys studying more than 1,500 obituaries in Ohio, and then from across the United States. In both samples, the study showed that men and women with documented religious affiliations lived an average of 9.45 and 5.64 years longer respectively than those who did not. Those statistics offer compelling evidence that being religious comes with a longevity boost.

Jamie Ducharme, a writer for *Time* Magazine, starts an article she wrote by asserting, "If a long life is what you're after, going to church may be the answer to your prayers."

Many years ago, I heard a speaker cite a study that was done at Johns Hopkins Hospital which said that those who prayed for others and are prayed for live longer. Don't press me for details because I do not remember the speaker or the name of the study, but I do remember what he said. Prayer works.

Being close to God offers countless enhancements to life. Getting a few extra years on earth is just the cherry on the sundae. It might be time well-spent to cozy up to God.

AM I IN THE WAY?

I spent a whole bunch of my life feeling as though most other people were conspiring to slow me down , get in my way, and waste my time. I was supercharged with energy and impatience. I resented the driver in front of me going the speed limit, the lady in front of me in the grocery store checkout line who insisted on having the clerk check her coupons and, inevitably, fumbled through her change purse looking for the exact change, and the chubby kid who was comatized with indecision about whether to buy Milk Duds, Junior Mints, or a Butterfinger at the theater refreshment counter. I had real difficulty understanding indecision, foot dragging, excessive timidity, and folks who seemed to be stuck in neutral. In general, most people were in my way.

Needless to say, I was a Type A personality, and probably still am. Thinking about it now, in my case, that "A" might have stood for "asshole." I suppose I held myself in awfully high esteem, or I would not have placed such a dear value on my time and importance. Truth is, I now realize I wasn't so special and wasn't in nearly as big of a hurry as I thought I was. I was used to living in a hurry, even when I wasn't in one. Old age has done a good job of teaching most of us that, in the final analysis, we are nothing more than average. Aging is humbling. I am now comforted in knowing that I am no longer expected to run…anywhere, anytime. Like everything else in my life, aging has affected my Type A personality. It has now sagged to about a Type B minus personality. Maybe getting us off our high horse is God's way of preparing us for the afterlife. I figure there's only room for one big shot in Heaven, and that spot is taken.

As golden agers, we are now the ones driving the speed limit, counting out our change to the grocery checker, and walking so slowly other pedestrians are stacking up behind us. When younger people ask us questions, they often have to ask us twice, because our hearing is deficient and we don't catch everything the first go around. In short, we are now the "load" (i.e., pain in the arse) that used to weight us down and drive us crazy. I hate that, but we can only play the cards God has dealt us.

Once in a while I catch a younger person just kind of watching me. I know it's not because I am handsome or famous. The face on the ogler usually has a somewhat pathetic look on their face, the kind that seems to say, "wow, that old boy has some rough miles on him." When I get a watcher, I wonder if they're counting the moles, warts, and age spots that now fight for space on my face, hands, and body. Is my zipper down? Spinach between my teeth? A dangling booger? Could it possibly be they find the strap lines that grace my cheeks thanks to my C-Pap machine attractive? I guess not. I sometimes wonder if God keeps a basket full of moles, warts, and age spots by His side, and, when He gets bored, He grabs a handful of those blemishes and hurls them at the elderly down on Earth. If so, His aim is far better than my ability to dodge those ugly missiles. It's possible that others sometime stare at us oldies for the same reason they stare at car wrecks and other disasters.

Another life span analogy I think about equates us humans to dogs. We all laugh at cute little puppies that are eager, clumsy, loving, and untrained. They are like we were when we were babies; cute, dependent, and irresponsible with our peeing and pooping. They then become adult dogs that run fast, fend off intruders, and give comfort to their masters. If I had been a dog, I would have been a greyhound that was hellbent on chasing the rabbit until I finally ran out of energy and my legs wore out. At that point, I, and other old folks, quit being greyhounds, and became pokey, lazy, Basset Hounds. A Basset has flabby, saggy skin, wrinkles, rheumy eyes, and a body that is the antithesis of athletic. Sound familiar? It's not a huge challenge for me to stand naked before a mirror and see a Basset Hound looking back at me.

As our life expectancy increases, so does society's need to deal with our more frequent illnesses and our staying on life's stage a longer time than needed. I read an article that said the men in England in 1841 could expect to live to the ripe old age of 40.2 years—women made it to 42.3. That same article said that in 1920 men in England lived to an average of 56 years (females 59). By 2019, England's men were hanging around to be 79.9 (females 83.6). See the trend? The longer you can live, the older you're apt to become before dying. Think about it.

The U. S. Census Bureau released a study in February of 2020 that projected that in 2060, men in the United States would live to 85.6 and women would make it to close to 90.

This demographic detour leaves little doubt that if we are in the way of the younger people now, they need to brace themselves. We are set on a path to just keep hanging around and getting in the way of others. As best I can figure, there are only two ways for us old folks to avoid being in the way: isolating ourselves or dying. Neither option gets me excited.

It is thrilling to see our children and grandchildren get their lives in gear and excel in what they do. While we rejoice in their successes and coping skills, they also remind us that our days of grabbing the brass ring are behind us. Being a happy oldster requires us to shake off our can't do's and focus on the pride we have in how the younger people have risen to meet their challenges.

"Fear not" appears in the Bible 365 times. As old people, we must continuously remind ourselves of this admonition, because getting old brings lots of scary things along with it. But, if we focus our thoughts and memories on the good parts of our lives, we, generally, find our asset column far exceeds out debit column. Life has given us so many blessings, our time is well spent remembering them, not dwelling on our woes, past battles, and what old age has taken from us. We have lots to smile about and we look better smiling than we do when frowning.

BEING OLD IS COMPLICATED

There are many subtleties involved with getting old that most younger folks don't notice in their aging family members and friends. Many of those subtle changes occur under the loosely defined banner of "complications." Over time, the cumulative effect of dealing with all of these complications can leave old-timers feeling overwhelmed by what used to be simple chores and figuring out how to deal with life's issues.

These complications don't assault the aging population in blitzkrieg style, barring major health setbacks such as strokes, loss of mobility, or impairment of brain functions. They are more like a slow-spreading virus that infects nearly all of our motor and mental skills over time. They tend to sneak up on us as we age and rob us of our coping skills one ability at a time. We are, more or less, helpless to stem this loss of "control" of our daily routines because the aging process is relentless, and it carries much of our self-confidence and independence away from us on its coattails.

In the beginning, many of our complications are rather minor and don't pose major impediments to our lifestyles. Maybe we struggle with getting the lid on our pickle jar off. Little chores like removing medicine bottle caps can end up being quite challenging, also. Or, perhaps, minor household repairs that require a little bit of hand strength, bending, or reaching, become vexing. Maybe we find our agility and dexterity are inferior to what they once were. I now find completing simple chores takes much longer than they once did. And, oh, before I forget to mention it, I cannot be the only oldster that sometimes struggles with understanding written instructions. I fear and suspect that many of them are written in Chinese and are poorly translated into English. Also, if they get the print size any smaller on most instructions, we will need electron microscopes to read them.

The gradual deterioration of physical and mental stamina and strength complicates and lengthens tasks that once were snaps. Even pushing a vacuum cleaner around can become physically taxing. I still don't have a hard time raking leaves, but it's bending over and loading the leaves into the bag I find difficult. Bending and returning to the erect position are not my friends. If I need to sit on the floor for some reason, I basically squat down and fall the rest of the way. My trying to get up looks like a Saturday Night Live skit. I roll, I grab, I push, I pull, and, in the end, usually require the assistance of someone else to stand back up. Once standing, I have to stay in neutral until my balance returns. Standing up too fast can produce dizziness. Truly, however, that is no longer a problem for me because I cannot stand up fast anymore.

The simple act of trimming my toenails has become a complicated operation. First of all, I can't see them clearly. I know they are at the end of my feet, but my bifocals fail to bring them into focus. They must reside at a distance somewhere between the two parts of my bifocals. Perhaps I need to go to my optometrist and have him fit me with trifocals, with the third "focal" designed to zoom in on my toes. Bending over to get closer to my toes puts bigtime pressure on my diaphragm which stops me from breathing. That same phenomenon occurs when I bend over to tie my shoes. Viva la loafers!

When I take a walk, I now go slowly and pay careful attention to where I put my feet. I am no longer in a rush to finish my walk in a timely fashion. I am more focused on just finishing the walk in the stand-up position. I have mastered the ability to turn a thirty-minute walk into an hour-long trek because, when old people fall, things like bones often break.

Putting make-up on often turns into a real job for women as they get old. While most of the troubles getting make-up on the right spots and in the right amounts can be blamed on diminished eyesight, dealing with skin that is no longer taut can be challenging, too. Flab must be harder to decorate, and unsteady hands make the application of make-up tricky. My wife, Kay, stuck a large magnifying mirror onto her normal mirror and it seemed to help. Bright lights over their mirrors aren't generally kind to older folks, but they do help in applying make-up.

Writing about make-up reminds me of something besides women's faces that have to be made up: beds. It may be a lousy transition from making up faces to making up beds, but it's the best I have. Due to a loss of strength, Kay now has a hard time putting the fitted sheets onto our king-sized bed. The process requires lifting the corners of the mattress and holding them long enough to stretch the elasticized sheet corners on them. Being the big strong husband I am, I told her I would help put the sheets on whenever needed. After assuming the job couldn't be very tough, I struggled mightily with lifting the mattress corners and holding them in place the required amount of time. Nowadays, when I hear the drier cut off, I pull a Houdini-inspired disappearing act so Kay will have to deal with that chore on her own. Who would have ever thought just putting on sheets could be such a complicated process?

The ability to be a good driver deteriorates as one gets long in the tooth. Many old drivers refuse to acknowledge they are no longer skilled helmsmen. Everyone around them knows they should take away their keys, but, instead, they let them continue to bounce off of curbs and bump into stuff in their way. I am not as good of a driver as I once was. Studies have shown that old people hang onto their ability to drive for as long as possible. They equate it to their personal freedom and they hate to deal with the thought of being totally dependent on others to get around. I understand that completely, but I also realize I will reach the point where I need to cede my keys to better drivers. My reflexes are still good, but I don't pay attention and my depth perception is a bit off. I don't talk on my phone when I'm driving, but I constantly take in the passing scenery as though I am afraid I might miss something. Unlike me, Kay has the ability to fully focus on her driving. She doesn't even turn her radio on when she's driving because it may distract her. She may miss a lot by focusing so hard on her driving but she's a better driver than me. It galls me to admit that.

As we age, we expect memory lapses, and they do come. I have organized my many medicines and supplements into day-of-the-week divided boxes. They work very well—when I remember to check them. I think I am doing a good job of staying on target with my medications, but, to my surprise, when I restock them, I often find I have forgotten to take a day's meds. For some weird reason, I am prone to skip my meds on Tuesdays or Wednesdays. Memory lapses (and losses) also affect our ability to recall people, things, numbers, and stuff. We inure to that condition over time and the older we get, the more people forgive us for our faulty recall.

Everyone, regardless of age, is besieged and frustrated by excessive paperwork. That statement is true, but it should be modified by adding that old people have a much tougher time handling the paperwork. First of all, understanding the government gobbledygook and words designed to stave off lawsuits are doubly difficult for golden agers. As we conceded in the previous paragraph, our memory sucks. Remembering where we filed the information being requested is a chore and remembering where we wrote down our passwords can add to our frustration.

Even contacting one's doctor is danged near impossible anymore. Many practices have set up computerized portals as mechanisms for communicating with your doctor, their physician's assistant, their nurse practitioner, their nurse, the scheduling assistant, or the janitor. Passwords and patience are required for this process to work. Someone needs to tell those people managing medical practices that telephones have been invented and they are quite efficient. We no longer have to fill out as much paperwork every time we visit our doctor. We just have to figure out how to fill it out on line before our visit. Even after doing that, they usually come up with other paperwork for you to complete when you arrive for your appointment.

There are numerous sources of paperwork that complicate an oldster's life. Social Security, Medicare, insurance companies, financial institutions, retirement fund managers, the IRS, utilities, and every organization or company you do business with that wants you to take a survey that records your experience as a customer, provide a steady stream of paperwork for you to complete and cuss about.

Since this chapter deals with some of the complications with which the elderly must contend, I just have to mention technology. It has been talked about in previous chapters, but, like it or not, it is a major contributor to the frustrations many, many oldsters encounter. My wife handles technology far better than I do. She may fuss and cuss about it sometimes, but she works with it. Me? I am destined to go through my remaining years in a dense technology fog; a fog I can't see through, navigate, or blow away.

Working with numbers can be a real rascal for us as we age. We know our numbers and many of us are better than average mathematicians. However, our confidence in our math and working with numbers is weakened with age and, honestly, we are prone to making more mistakes than we did when younger. That tendency causes us to check our work over and over and, it's not unusual for us to re-add a column of numbers three times and come up with three totals. We just have to keep doing it over and over until the right answer repeats itself. Checking and re-checking our work is quite time consuming, but it has become the necessary norm.

Most old folks are pretty trusting of those with whom they do business. They pretty well have to trust others because they have no choice. It's not surprising so many elderly people get scammed by unscrupulous contractors, roofers, mechanics, salesmen, driveway repairmen, car dealerships, plumbers, and electricians. The dishonest vendors prey on the old and rely on their trust to pull off the scam. They are also assholes. Your best bet is to pray for honest repairmen and salesmen. Your second best option is to carry a gun and use it on those who cheat you. Now, to be fair and accurate, most vendors are honest folks hellbent on doing you a good job that is fairly priced. Checking references will help you find the good ones. You might even want to ask for a copy of their license and take a photo of the vendor.

For every negative feature of getting old, there is an offsetting positive feature. I have always been amazed at how many people are eager to help those in need of assistance. It's a mistake for old people to shy away from asking for help. Do it. If you have a problem, there is probably a government program available to help you solve it. Churches will help. Give others a chance to feel good about themselves and ask for their help if you need it. Life is not so complicated when others help.

Another source of help for "believers" is God. Prayer is our conduit to Him, and if you are like me, your praying habits and prayer contents have changed with age.

When I was a kid, I prayed the bumps on my face would "clear up" before the big dance. As an old fellow, I pray the bumps on my face are non-cancerous.

When I was a kid I prayed I would pass my college entrance exam. As an old fellow, I pray I pass Heaven's entrance exam.

When I was a kid, I prayed my farts (poots, if you prefer) would be odorless or that the guy sitting next to me would be blamed if they weren't. As an old fellow, I pray my poots are just poots.

When I was a kid, I prayed the police wouldn't ticket me for speeding. As an old fellow, I pray the police won't ticket me for driving too slowly.

When I was a kid, I prayed for relief from all of the minor problems and nuisances that complicated my life. As an old man, I pray only for serious issues challenging my life and the lives of my loved ones and friends.

Praying has been a part of my life as long as I can recall thanks to a mother who had me say my prayers each night. That prayer may bring back memories to some of you seniors. It went:

Now I lay me down to sleep,
and pray dear Lord my soul to keep.
If I should die before I wake,
I pray dear Lord my soul to take.
God bless…(name each family member.)
Amen.

Mother would be pleased to know I still pray each night. My prayers are different now and because I am old and running a bit short of time, I now pray in ALL CAPS.

WHAT 84 SEPTUAGENARIANS AND OLDER FOLKS THINK

A lot of research went into the content of this book. It was fun to broaden my knowledge about the aging process, but I kept wondering if other older people had the same feelings, preferences, and memories I had. The magnitude of a project that really dug in to those questions was intimidating and above my pay scale. I lowered my sight and decided to do a survey of about 100 people who were seventy or older that would be fun and interesting. It wasn't an academic exercise, but it was fun and, I believe, yielded some interesting answers. The complete survey appears in the Appendix section at the book's end.

The first question on the survey was: "Other than your health and that of your loved ones, what do you worry most about?" The top five worries my 84 responders selected were:

1. the move toward Socialism in America;
2. the moral decay of Society;
3. disrespect for the law;
4. illegal immigration; and,
5. organized religions' diminished influence on the family unit.

Not one person checked "world peace" and only five checked "terrorism." One responder indicated "nothing" on the survey. I believe he or she figured out how to live out their remaining years without letting worries drag them down. Now, if I were a betting man, I would lay money on that guy or gal to outlive the rest of us.

Question #2 asked, "Do you think life is more complex for younger generations than what you have experienced?" Eighty-seven per cent (87%) of those responding, said "yes." That doesn't surprise me since people today have to make decisions in an environment that is always eight and one-half months pregnant with conflicting information. Technological advancements and a rampaging social media that, too often, seems to feed on fanning differences rather than striving for tolerance and unity add to the complexities with which young people must cope.Only three responders thought that things today are about the same for young people as they were for us old folks.

Question #3 asked the surveyed, "Who is/was your favorite television detective?" I gave them a list of 36 tv shamuses from which to choose, and here were the top five vote getters:

1. Columbo (Peter Falk)
2. Rockford (James Garner)
3. Magnum (Tom Selleck)
4. Joe Friday (Jack Webb)
5. Sherlock Holmes (several actors, beginning with Basil Rathbone)

At least one of the golden agers that completed the survey still has a grand sense of humor. He or she wrote in: Barney Fife!

Question #4 asked, "Who was your favorite television doctor?"
The top four vote getters were:

1. Marcus Welby (Robert Young—by a big margin)
2. House (Hugh Laurie)
3. Dr. Kildare (Richard Chamberlain)
4. Ben Casey (Vince Edwards)

Question #5 simply asked, "Mason or Matlock?" In a close race, Mason beat Matlock by eight votes. I would be delighted to be represented by either fellow.

Question #6 got a bit more serious, and asked responders: "Which of the following presidents do you think were the most effective?" Our choices were limited to Franklin Roosevelt and those who have served since he did. Here are the top five vote getters:

1. Ronald Reagan (by a whopping landslide)
2. Franklin Roosevelt
3. Donald Trump (he did not demand a recount)
4. Dwight Eisenhower
5. Harry Truman.

John Kennedy was a close 6th, but some of the fellows struck out. Here are the five worst vote getters from worst to fifth worst:

1. Jimmie Carter
2. Joe Biden
3. Gerald Ford
4. Richard Nixon
5. Bill Clinton

After reading the responses, I can attest to the fact that some folks are angry about our current state of politics. One voter was nasty in his or her remarks about Trump, while a few made some unkind comparisons between Biden and certain animals.

Question #7 asks responders to "Name your three favorite sports stars of all time." This question revealed a wide array of choices. It seems everyone has their own favorites and reaching a consensus was dang near impossible. However, when all of votes were counted, the following three stars were the winners:

1. Roger Staubach (football)
2. Tiger Woods (golf)
3. Mickey Mantle (baseball)

Babe Ruth and Michael Jordan showed well but couldn't catch the three winners.

A number of women received votes. The top three female vote getter were:

1. Billie Jean King (tennis)
2. Babe Didrikson Zaharias (golf, track, and tennis)
3. A tie between: Peggy Fleming (ice skating) and Mary Lou Retton (gymnastics).

Question #8 also drew a lot of different answers. It asked for those responding to name their three favorite male movie stars. The top five favorites were:

1. John Wayne (won easily)
2. Paul Newman

3. Clint Eastwood

4. Tom Hanks

5. Jimmy Stewart

I suspect the one who voted for Roy Rogers as his favorite had a happy childhood and is still living in the past. The one who selected Bing Crosby probably croons in the shower.

Question #9 asked those surveyed to "Name your three favorite female stars of all time," Consensus was hard to find, but the following five stars took top honors:

1. Meryl Streep

2. Katherine Hepburn

3. Julia Roberts

4. Audrey Hepburn

5. Liz Taylor.

Sandra Bullock made a strong showing as did Julie Andrews.

Question 10 asked those taking the survey to: "Name the three comedians/comediennes who made you laugh the most." The winners were:

1. Red Skelton

2. Tim Conway

3. Lucille Ball

4. A tie for 4th between Bob Hope and Rodney Dangerfield (he finally got some respect).

Steve Martin, Carol Burnett, and Jerry Seinfeld came close to cracking the top five. I find it funny that two redheads were in the top three.

Question #11 then asked, "Do you nap daily?"

Fifty-four per cent (54%) said "no", with the remaining forty-six percent (46%) answering yes. Some noteworthy trends popped up here. Eighty-one percent (81%) of those admitting to napping were men, while seventy-two per cent (72%) of those saying they did not take naps were women. I can think of lots of reasons men feel tired enough daily to nap, but I can't figure out why women aren't equally tired. Could it be that living with women wears a fellow out?

Question #12—the last question in the survey—asked, "Who was/is your favorite television talk show host/hostess?"

Well, "Here's Johnny!" Johnny Carson ran away with the vote. He received over 90% of the first place votes. Only five responders cast a first-place vote for someone other than Carson. Steven Colbert received three votes, while Steve Allen and David Letterman each got one.

Conan O'Brien and Dave Garraway tied for last place. Others who flopped in the poll were:

- Joey Bishop
- Jon Stewart
- Ellen DeGeneres; and,
- Jimmy Kimmel

I'm fairly certain this survey will not be republished by academia. Sometimes it's just fun to go off the rails of convention. Enjoy the results of this survey, but don't base your dissertation on it.

AS THE END NEARS

No matter how many nice things we say about getting old; no matter how much fun we try to make the golden years sound; no matter how much exercise we do, and no matter how many anti-aging pills and supplements we take or facelifts we have; we all face the same final chapter. We die. That comes as no surprise for any of us, but sometimes finishing out our lives is akin to finishing a book when we know how it ends—not much fun. Coming to terms with death seems far easier for those of us who believe in life after death. It gives us hope/faith that we will be reunited with loved ones who have gone on before us. That feeling or belief is comforting indeed. At the very minimum, that belief makes it much easier to accept our earthly mortality.

As we start preparing ourselves for life's end, we start trying to organize our final chapter. Personally, I do not dwell on finishing a lot of tasks before I die, but I do sometimes lay in bed and think about exactly what I want to take care of while I am still breathing. There are messes I need to clean up and loose ends I need to trim. I do not want to take any unsaid "I love you" or unsaid "thank you" to the grave with me. I want to say them all and leave on a positive and upbeat note. Death has a way of being permanent, and anything left undone, or even under-done, remains that way forever. Dying is never far from our thoughts, and I, personally, look at some people and some things wondering if it will be the last time I will see them. When I am with my children or grandchildren, I find myself almost straining to commit their images and personalities to my memory. I really don't know why I feel this need to commit them to memory deep down inside of me. It's unlikely I will be able to take those memories with me when I die. I will surely leave a few memories, but unfortunately, probably won't be able to take any with me. What a waste.

We should all want to leave a trail of love behind us when we die that connects us to all of the people who have been important to us. We want to leave a soothing scent of kindness that uplifts those who have known us. Mother Theresa said many, many quotable things, but my favorite was, "Do small things with large love." I have never found a reason to be stingy with love. Old age has taught me that love is a healing wonder drug that should be liberally spread around our world, a world that always has its share of aches, pains, sorrows, and needs.

The desire to leave life on our terms may be Pollyannaish, but, at this point in our lives, why would we want to "go out" any other way? Old age is the time—the only time—left for us to right any wrongs we may have committed, extend any apologies that are in order, and to muster a strong rally to end our time on earth with a flourish of goodness. People may not remember exactly what we did or said, but they will always remember how we made them feel. Prepping for our own death is not limited to getting our spiritual houses in order. We have to get other things in order, too; things like living wills and wills instructing folks on who gets what when we move on, assuming there is a what. Winston Churchill, a witty wordsmith, supposedly said, "Where there's a will, I want to be in it." Sorry, Winston, you are not in mine.

We studied Thornton Wilder's three act play, "Our Town", in high school. In it, Wilder created the mythical village of Grover's Corner, New Hampshire. In act III, Emily has died but chooses to revisit Grover's Corner to relive one of her favorite days from her life—her twelfth birthday. In her short time back on earth, she realizes how little people appreciate the simple joys of life. She further realizes that every moment of life should be treasured. When she asked the stage manager (the narrator) if anyone truly understands the value of life while they live it, he responds, "No. The saints and poets, maybe—they do some." "Our Town" won a Pulitzer Prize, and the lesson it teaches is clearly worthy of our contemplation.

"Our Town" was written in 1938. In 1973, another play dealing with death made its debut off Broadway. It was entitled "Steambath," by Bruce Jay Friedman. The play never won a Pulitzer and, to my knowledge, is not taught in high school, but it did have an unusual take on death. It begins with a few people waking up in a steambath in New York City that has no easy exit. Eventually, it becomes clear to them that the steambath is a sort of afterlife where indifferent souls come to tell their stories to God. God happens to be the attendant picking up the towels. He is a short-tempered God who refuses to perform miracles just to prove who he is. The steambath is referred to as a waiting room for heaven. The only thing I took from the play was that maybe we'll all show up at a steambath in New York on our way to heaven. Remember, if we do, we should all be extra nice to the attendant. Simply stated, we don't know exactly where death will take us or the route it will take in getting us there. We, also, don't know what God looks like.

End times is an opportunity to use all of our life's experiences to separate the wheat from the chaff; a time to decide what of life is worth savoring and what was nothing more than peripheral piffle. Novelist C.J. Box had a crusty old character that said, "I've been around the block so many times my tires are bald." I have, too, crusty old character, and I know I wasted a lot of life's miles going in those circles. If we have accumulated any wisdom in our many years, it's time to put it to work. Death will be more tolerable if we can die feeling as though we figured out many of the great things life afforded us. It's better, I think, than dying dumb.

It makes sense that we should try to live our lives in such ways that allow us to look behind us with satisfaction. When we look behind us, we should do so knowing and acknowledging we have made mistakes. However, we should try to minimize future mistakes and keep them as small as is possible. If we are not careful, spending too much time looking behind us and spinning around to look ahead of us can make us dizzy and prove to be confusing. American author, spiritualist, and guru Baba Ram Dass advised to , "Be here, now!" He admonished us to avoid spending too much time in the past or the future, meaning "now" is where the action is.

We have all seen older people who have been swallowed-up by the sadness that comes with the losses they have suffered along life's way. They appear to be laboring under a weight that is more than they can manage. The light in their eyes is dim and they often seem to be just waiting for life to leave them. Most all of us have moments we feel the cumulative effects of losses we have experienced, but the lucky—or smart—among us shake off their blues and find the strength to re-focus their lives to the joy love adds to their being. They still know there remain traces of Eden with us and that peace is reborn in us each day. They seem to be able—at least partially—to offset the losses they have suffered by adding new people to love, new activities in which to engage, and good to do for others. If we watch them closely, we learn that loving others is the manna that nourishes their souls and ours alike. It is the power source for that little light that burns inside of us and lights our path. It is the nutrient that feeds the quality of our lives and keeps us vital.

Whether we dash through the years, skip through life, or waddle through life, we interact with thousands and thousands of people on the same pilgrimage. The previously quoted spiritualist, Ram Dass, once said, "We are all just walking each other home." That quote conjures up a nice image, as the shared mission of walking each other home unifies us in our singular goal, that of going home. It is far easier to walk down that dark lane if we know home is at its end.

Each person we encounter on our trip through life contributes to what and who we become in our time. Some encounters are very brief, but even those add a pinch of themselves to the recipe for the concoction that becomes us. Logic tells us that longer encounters with fellow travelers produce greater influences on us than those who pop in and out of our worlds. Parents, close friends, boyfriends and girlfriends, co-workers, teachers, ministers, classmates, spouses, and other family members all contribute to the ultimate us. We can make a fairly complete list of those who were our major influencers at different stages of our lives. It's more fun to think of those who were positive influences on us, but to be accurate, not all of those who contributed to our being added good things to the mix. Along with the sugar and sweetness, I can rattle off a number of individuals who laced my life with vinegar, bad habits, and harmful ingredients I would have been better off taking a pass on.

At this point in my life, all of those good and bad contributions to the man I have become have fermented and taken root in my body, mind, and soul and left me with being me. Few of us are completely satisfied with who we are. We are usually very hard on ourselves and tend to wallow in our unworthiness. Dass said, "Your problem is that you are too busy holding on to your unworthiness." I suspect all of us feel as though we could have done better in life, been better in life, and been worth more to our fellow man, In judging ourselves, we skip right over the fact that we are imperfect creatures, filled with faults, inadequacies, laziness, and selfish tendencies. The great "bail-out" that is available to us is that our requests for forgiveness will be granted by our loving God. If we believe in the power of forgiveness and the happiness that comes from shedding those heavy burdens of guilt, we will know the pleasure of gliding—not plodding—through life. Bishop Tutu gave us something to think about when he said, "There is no future without forgiveness." I did read a saying that was obviously written by a skeptic. It said, "A clear conscience is the sign of a fuzzy memory." I guess there could be some truth to that.

Now seems to be the appropriate time to remind ourselves that, in spite of our shortcomings, God loves us. If God loves us, we must be lovable.

WHAT HAPPENS WHEN WE DIE?

Most of us are curious about what happens to us when we die. Afterall, we do have a vested interest. What really happens to us is a bit of a mystery, well, okay, a very big one. Believers in an afterlife think (and hope) death on Earth brings a rebirth, a new life that is charged with goodness and love and spent in the presence of God. They believe we simply transfer to another place, perhaps in a different form. While even the most devout Christians can't agree on the details of what the afterlife is like, there does seem to be a consensus that we are going to love it. Religious doubters and the unimaginative think that when we die, we are simply interred and dissolve into the dirt after a while. That theory is not fun and leaves no room for hope. Personally, I believe Heaven is in my future, and I find it comforting to believe Heaven comes with a guarantee of love and happiness forever. Let's hope that's the case.

Some folks who buy into the afterlife idea believe it will be very difficult to gain entrance into Heaven, while others think since Jesus died on the cross for our sins, we'll get a free pass. A preacher friend of mine believes God will accept all of us into Heaven, but that some of us may have to stand in the corner for a while.

Ask ten people who plan on going to Heaven what they think it will be like, and you are likely to get ten different answers. Not knowing exactly what Heaven will be like allows each of us to "design" ourselves a Heaven that is as we would have it be. My Heaven is one in which we all recognize each other and get to do lots of hugging, kissing, and loving with those we have loved on earth. Won't it be fun sharing this pain free, worry free, perfect place with loved ones and friends? In my Heaven, we will see God and get to know Him, and He will reveal to us all of the secrets about how He operates. We will live in a state of constant awe.

This concept of Heaven being "perfect" and "eternal" does give me some angst though. I'm not completely sold on living in a place where everyone has a perfect singing voice, no one ever has a skinned knee, never makes a bogie, and always hits a homerun in the angel softball game. I can't imagine going fishing where you always catch trophy fish. Will we all have the same I.Q. in Heaven?

My friend, Don Jones, who is a retired minister, says he's not completely excited by the concept of eternal life. He says he can't imagine doing anything for an eternity. At the risk of putting words in his mouth, I would venture to guess his version of Heaven comes with an expiration date stamped on it.

My wife, Kay, thinks when we die, we are changed into little flashes of light that flit through Heaven mixing with other souls (lights) and loving everyone. After giving her concept some thought, I told her to watch over her shoulder, because I will be trailing her to make sure she's not blinking her light at some other blinking guy. I don't want her to be light flirting while she is flitting.

Tuck Kemper, a dear friend since the first grade, likens Heaven to sitting inside an IMAX theater every day and watching God's slide show that explains how He created the world and all of its creatures. Each day, He will amaze us with revelations about His power and how He has used it so far. Now, Tuck's vision of Heaven is far more thoughtful and complex than having a front row seat in the Lord's IMAX theatre, but I like this twist on it. He's not certain if popcorn will be served, but he knows it will be a great show.

Devote some quiet time to design your own version of Heaven. Whatever you come up with can become the carrot at the end of the stick as you approach the end of your Earth-life. Put your design in your hope chest and hang on to it.

Others think that after we die, we will all just hang around in some unknown state or place until Judgement Day. On that day, we will stand before God and listen to his decision about whether we are admitted into Heaven or put on the elevator that goes to the basement. That possibility comes with some advice. If we're going to stand before God while He reviews our file and decides our fate, we would be well-advised to stand before Him with a good record.

This is as good of a place as any for me to remind you again that the drama that plays out after death is a huge mystery. I don't know whose version – if anyone's – will prove the closest to reality, but I struggle with the idea that God will choose winners and losers from His very own creations. I am so glad He is in charge.

If you are older and have children or grandchildren, I know you have worried about their future after you die. Our desire to take care of our loved ones doesn't stop when we are bogged down in old age. We love them so much we just can't stand the thought of not being there for them in their times of need. In truth, they probably don't need us nearly as much as we need to be needed by them.

One way to handle not knowing what happens when we die, is to not die. Of course, avoiding death is not possible, but it might be possible to put it off for some time simply by relocating. According to BBC.com, in Japan, the average age of those dying is eighty-three, and if you live on Okinawa or another of the small islands near it, you can probably beat that eighty-three figure. That little group of islands is called "the land of immortals" because so many old people just keep hanging on. Though small in physical size, Okinawa and the small cluster of islands are home to more than four-hundred centenarians. Credit for their longevity is given to the local diet, which includes plentiful tofu and sweet potato, and a small amount of fish. Plus, they are very short.

In Spain, the average death age is 82.8. Experts credit the fact that business stops every day from 2 pm to 5 pm for siesta and the fact that they are height-challenged. I could get into that siesta stuff, but I am well over six-foot tall so it's too late for me to be short.

Singapore residents, who are also short, have an average death age of eighty-three. Strong medical facilities and a healthcare system that focuses on preventive care are cited as the principal reasons for their longevity.

Switzerland boasts the world's highest average death age for men at eighty-one. Access to top quality healthcare and a sense of well-being help keep Swiss men alive longer than those of most countries. Also, there is very little poverty in Switzerland, and, oh yes, they avoid wars and world politics.

South Korea has been pegged by the experts to become the first country that will hit the life expectancy age of ninety. Per Camille Hoheb of Wellness Tourism Worldwide, "South Koreans' diet, which is rich in fermented foods are said to lower cholesterol, boost immunity, and inhibit cancer." In the article published by BBC Hoheb added. "As a whole, Korean food is high in fiber and nutrient dense." The article said, "Residents say a cultural focus on community and the associate traditions contributes to the everyday quality of life." Hoheb summed up her take on why South Koreans may be enjoying greater longevity than many societies by saying, "In South Korea there's also an overall sense of mindfulness that comes with the Buddhist mindset and an overall attitude toward a culture of cooperation versus individualism." (26) Now, before you move to South Korea, you should know that "fermented foods" does not mean booze.

It's funny to me that exercise is not credited with adding to longevity in any of the five countries with the highest average death age. My guess is that couch potatoes wrote those articles. Diet, on the other hand, gets lots of credit. I could get used to the new diets if I relocated, but I would sure miss chicken fried steaks, gravy, and Blue Bell Ice Cream.

All of the research in the world won't lead to the answer about what happens when we die. As we said earlier, the only way to find out what really happens when we die is to die, but most of us don't mind waiting a while.

I run the risk of making mistakes as I try to enumerate a few of the disparate beliefs of some of the major religions about their beliefs regarding what happens after death, but I'm going to try it anyway. Be reminded there is one Bible, yet thousands of denominations differ on their interpretations of it. Also, no descriptions of a religion, a denomination, or either's teachings are practiced by their full memberships. Because there are so many who stray from the strict confines of the "ism" they profess to practice, simple definitions of their belief systems are dangerous and incomplete. Most are mushy at their edges, so keep that in mind when you read what I have written about their beliefs on what happens when they die. In spite of these disclaimers and acknowledgements of the presence of believers who stray, I have copied the different religions' positions on post-death directly from what they published in their own literature.

I remember a cult called Heaven's Gate founded by Marshall Applewhite in the 1990s. While Applewhite never realized his dream of building a huge following, he did talk thirty-nine people into a mass suicide in 1997. According to Wikipedia, Applewhite convinced his band of followers that they would be visited by extraterrestrials who would transplant their souls into new bodies and take them all to heaven on the tail of a comet. I really feel sorry for those people that bought into Applewhite's fantasy. It is probable they weren't handling life on Earth very well. To be fair, I should point out that I really don't know whether the thirty-nine bodies were loaded onto a comet by aliens and hauled off to a distant star. However, if your preacher tells you we're going to Heaven on a comet's tail, find a new preacher.

According to hinduamerican.com, the Hindu faith is centered around reincarnation, and that their souls are recycled repeatedly until they settle upon their true nature. This cycle of death and rebirth is called samsara.

Buddhism believes that the actions of a person lead to a new existence after death in an endless cycle. This cycle is considered to be unsatisfactory and painful. The cycle only stops if moksha (liberation) is achieved by insight into the extinguishing of craving.

Judaism is famously ambiguous about what happens after death, so I will leave it at that. Since they didn't buy into the resurrection of Jesus, they've never felt the need to address the question of an afterlife.

Islam believes in an afterlife. In fact, it's one of their six articles of faith. They believe it will be revealed by God whether they go to Heaven or to Hell at the time of their resurrection.

The website offthelefteye.com (27) offers an answer to the question of what happens after death. They say, "We go through five elements of what happens when we die. The five elements are based upon the firsthand account of Emanuel Swedenborg", a Swedish theologian who died for real in 1772. The five elements are:

- an unconditionally loving welcome;
- you will still be you, but the deeper you;
- you will be free to go wherever you want to go;
- you will have a life review; and,
- you will have opportunities to learn and progress.

I am not certain how Swedenborg experienced these five elements or how he communicated his findings to his followers. Perhaps, he died and then returned to life, as many others have reported doing. All of these thoughts and doctrines are just part of the big mystery.

In 1982, a Gallup survey indicated that eight million adults in the United States had undergone a near-death experience (28). The people sampled reported having some of the following ten "happenings" during their episode, eight of which appear to be unique to near-death experiences. Here are the ten:

- out of body experience;
- accurate visual perception while out of body;
- accurate auditory perception while out of body;
- feelings of peace and painlessness;
- light phenomena—encounter with loving white light;
- life review;
- being in another world;
- encountering other beings;
- tunnel experience; and,
- precognition.

This near-death phenomenon has been reported enough to make believers of many people. There are numerous similarities between most of the stories we hear from those who have experienced near-death. All things considered, I might be one of those believers—haven't decided for sure. At any rate, it's one more reason to put hope on our horizon.

Dr. Richard Wing told me he did not enjoy Alfred Hitchcock's movie, "The Birds," because it left too many unanswered questions at the end. He said Rod Taylor and Tippi Hedren just drove away at the end, leaving lots of birds watching them do so. These were the same birds that had tried to peck their eyes out and wreaked havoc throughout the town. Dr. Wing, to this day, wants to know what caused the birds to turn angry and aggresive. He felt unfulfilled. He will have to ask Alfred Hitchcock that question when he gets to Heaven. I'm afraid that if Dr. Wing reads this chapter of my book expecting it to be neatly ended with mystery-solving answers, he will be unfulfilled again; it doesn't.

Hope and optimism were put into the hearts and minds of man by our Creator for a reason. With practice, we can learn to adjust our beliefs and attitudes by infusing those wonderful attributes into our very being. We can design a very happy answer to that question because Christianity gives us the freedom to believe in happy endings, and I do. I do not fear death, but I more or less agree with Woody Allen who said, "I'm not afraid of dying; I just don't want to be there when it happens." Amen, Woody.

A HODGEPODGE OF FINAL THOUGHTS

Unless an unexpected brainstorm hits me, this is the last chapter of this book. As I went back through my countless notes, I found a number of things I wished I had worked into the manuscript. None of them deserve chapter status, but they are worthy of mention. Don't look for threads that will tie the various subjects together. There aren't any; hence the word "hodgepodge" in the title of this chapter.

I researched whether or not people who retired early shortened their life span and it appears the consensus is they do. An article that appeared on the website elderguru.com (29) said that…"and in general, people who retired at age 55 are 89% more likely to die within three years than those who retire at age 65. We should point out that most of those taking early retirement are less educated than those who wait for full retirement age and probably have more unhealthy lifestyles."

A study of Shell Oil Company retirees concluded that those who retired at age 55 and lived to be 65, died 37% sooner than those who retired at 65. The Social Security Administration noticed that trend, as well. Their conclusion was that men who retire at age 62 have a 20% higher likelihood of death than the general population. It is interesting, however, that for women retiring early there is no increase in their mortality rate. Apparently, women maintain much more active social and lifestyle activities than their male counterparts.

I have fought the urge to preach to younger people about my version of what they need to do to live better lives. I'm just full of "you oughtas" trying to get out, but I decided they wouldn't listen any more than I would have when I was their age. It has, also, crossed my mind that I might be totally unqualified to give meaningful advice.

If I had talked to the younger folks, I would have seriously questioned their good sense when it came to tattoos. They will not age well and are seen—by this old codger—as stains on otherwise beautiful people. I will die not understanding that fad. No matter. The horse is out of the barn on tattoos. I would then try to convince them they are letting a whole lot of life escape their notice by staring down at their phones all of the time. Much of the information one can access on their phone is wonderful. Social media?

Not on my list of worthwhile stuff. I would also like to tell the younger folks to get the earbuds out of their ears and listen to the world. I would ask kids if they really like rap music. I can't stand it. In that regard, my dad used to ask me if I really liked the music of Elvis, Chubby Checker, Chuck Berry, and Little Richard. Of course I did. He couldn't stand it and was mystified by its popularity. Old people have no business telling young people what music to like. Lastly, I would suggest to young people that they study the wisdom of old people and learn from it. I read somewhere that when an old person dies, a library closes. Granted, some of old libraries had a lot of empty shelves.

If you've read the preceding chapters, you know I have used lists extensively. I've used them for fun and for an efficient way to share solid information. Unfortunately, I had some leftover items that should have appeared on some list. Here are some for your reading enjoyment:

- anonymous quote: "Life may not be the party we hoped for, but while we are here, we might as well dance."
- you know you are old if you wonder when they started letting children become policemen, firemen, and teachers;
- one good thing about getting old: my supply of brain cells is finally down to a manageable size;
- you know you are getting old if getting "lucky" now means you found your car in the parking lot;
- I used to be indecisive. Now, I'm not so sure;
- to be sure of hitting the target, shoot first and call whatever you hit the target;
- the last thing I want to do is hurt you, but it's still on my list;
- since light travels faster than sound, some people appear bright until you hear them speak;
- the only difference between a rut and a grave is the depth; and,
- if all is not lost, where the hell is it?

Writing a disjointed chapter like this makes me feel a little like Kurt Vonnegut. He sometimes thumbed his nose at convention and wrote in a style that defied comprehension. It, also, had to be fun for Lewis Carroll to pen "Jabberwocky", a nonsensical poem he wrote and included in his 1871 novel, Through the Looking Glass. It's liberating to write for the fun of writing, unincumbered by a fear of following good writing rules.

Perplexed by whether I should end this this book with a surge of humor, or whether I should wrap our end times in a serious thought or reminder, I decided to do both.

I leave you with a ditty inspired by the fact that aging keeps us ever-changing. Whenever asked how he was doing, my dear friend from Norman, Oklahoma, Bob Thompson, always answered, "I feel more like I do now than I did a while ago." After scratching my head many times in search of what he meant, I finally decided Bob knew of what he spoke

As an attempt at concluding this book on a serious and comforting note, I offer the sermon given by Henry Scott-Holland (1847-1918), a priest at St. Paul's Cathedral of London, while the body of King Edward VII was lying in state at Westminster. It is a wonderful way to think of death, the only cure for aging:

Death is nothing at all.
It does not count.
I have only slipped away into the next room.
Nothing has happened.

Everything remains exactly as it was.
I am I, and you are you,
And the old life that we lived so fondly together is untouched, unchanged.
Whatever we were to each other, that we are still.
Call me by the old familiar name.
Speak of me in the easy way which you always used.
Put no difference into your tone.
Wear no forced air of solemnity or sorrow.

Laugh as we always laughed at the little jokes that we enjoyed together.
Play, smile, think of me, pray for me.
Let my name be ever the household word that it always was.
Let it be spoken without an effort, without the ghost of a shadow upon
   it.
Life means all that it ever meant.
It is the same as it ever was.
There is absolute and unbroken continuity.
What is this death but a negligible accident?

Why should I be out of mind because I am out of sight?
I am but waiting for you, for an interval,
Somewhere very near,
Just around the corner.

All is well.
Nothing is hurt; nothing is lost.
One brief moment and all will be as it was before.
How we shall laugh at the trouble of parting when we meet again!

Final thought: I wish growing old had taken longer.

NOTES

1. James Lee Burke, "Every Cloak Rolled in Blood", Simon and Schuster, 2022.

2. Brenda Lee, "One Step At A Time", recording, RCA Records, 1974.

3. Mistupd.com. owned by *On Line Knowledge* Magazine article, "25 Signs You Are Getting Old."

4. Natalie Romero Of Ontario, CA article, "Ten Unmistakable Signs You Are Getting Old."

5. The Coventry Telegraph (England) article, "The Top 50 Signs You're Old."

6. Cafemom.com owned by Wild Sky Media, quotes from children about questions they want to ask God.

7. Lists regarding aging from websites of *National Institute of Health, Micro Health LLC, Web MD*, and mom.junction.com. P. 26.

8. Healthline.com website owned by Red Ventures; list of the 12 drugs they believe help extend longevity.

9. The Long Island Weight Loss Institute article, "What Foods Speed Up the Aging Process."

10. List of major causes of death in the U.S. in 2020 published by: CDC, NCHS, AHA, and the Washington State Health Care Authority.

11. Michael Watson, Director of Livable Communities at AARP, article identifying the seven traits shared by those living long lives.

12. Cyndi Fink interview published by *Quora* in article entitled "Some of The Best Qualities of Elderly People."

13. Study by *A Place for Mom* appearing on their website, aplaceformom.com. identifying what younger people thought about old people. P. 84

14. "Ageism Alive and Well in Advertising" article that appeared in AARP's bulletin, September 2021.

15. Federal Reserve's Survey of Consumer Finance.

16. Bureau of Labor Statistics, U.S. Department of Labor.

17. Mike Hodin, CEO of Global Coalition on Aging. _.

18. Kathy Mattea, "Where've You Been?", song written by Don Henry and Joe Venzer and released in 1989 by Mercury Records.

19. Numerous quotes from Richard Lederer, author of 60 books on words.

20. The Heritage At Brentwood's Senior Living newsletter article entitled, "Nine Things That Get Better With Age."

21. Littlethings.com website article, "Eleven Things That Improve With Age."

22. Men'shealth.com research on the effects of being tall on longevity.

23. Albert Einstein College of Health research on how one's height affects their likelihood of getting cancer. .

24. Social Anthropologist Brian Palmer's article on slate.com/Slate Magazine on height's affects on longevity.

25. Mayoclinic.org of the Mayo Clinic article by Clinic staff regarding benefits of a positive attitude for one's health.

26. Camille Hoheb, Wellness Tourism Worldwide, article published by BBC on South Korea's trend toward increased longevity.

27. Offthelefteye.com, website of the Swedenborg Foundation, article quoting the writing of Emanuel Swedenborg on near-death experiences.

28. Gallup Poll results published in 1982 regarding near-death experiences of those interviewed.

29. Elderguru.com article regarding the effects of early retirement on longevity.

Printed in the USA
CPSIA information can be obtained
at www.ICGtesting.com
LVHW091317250824
789126LV00005B/47